Nothing Ever Goes
On Here

To Lynn,
What a joy to
Get to know you!

Nothing Ever Goes On Here

A Memoir

Ellen Newhouse

With light, love & Gratitude,
xo Ellen
10.23.14

New Media Publications

Nothing Ever Goes On Here
A Memoir

Ellen Newhouse

F I R S T   E D I T I O N

Hardcover ISBN: 9781939288714

Paperback ISBN: 9781939288721

eBook ISBN: 9781939288752

Library of Congress Control Number: 2014943073

©2014 New Media Publications

www.EllenNewhouse.com

Published by New Media Publications,
An Imprint of Wyatt-MacKenzie

New Media Publications

Dedication

For Jim,
Whose enduring love and gentle nudges allowed me
to face myself, my doubts and all of my fears
on those blank empty pages.

Acknowledgments

To my astounding writing coach, Caroline Allen, without whose encouragement, patience and belief in me this book would never have come to fruition. Thank you for your friendship and your amazing ability to create the space that allowed me to recover and discover my own voice.

To my amazing writer's group—Emily Bumble, Lisa Favero, Leslie Gifford, Lori Hubbard and Jessica Muffett—whose honest and fierce feedback made me dig deep and become a much better writer.

Chad and Susan Smith, thank you for your enthusiasm and editing savvy.

Dixie Coskie, I am deeply grateful for our soul friendship, then and now. Thank you for your encouragement with my book and for your generosity of spirit. Who knew when we finished each other's poems so many years ago, we'd meet again and you would help me to bring my writing to fruition.

Nancy Cleary, how can I begin to thank you for honoring my book with your outstanding design work that spoke my heart and soul.

To my parents for being the most difficult teachers I will ever encounter who ultimately shaped who I have become. Dad, may your heart and soul find the peace I know you are searching for. Mom, I am so happy that you finally found love.

To my brothers and sister who may never understand the love that I have for all of them. Just know I love you.

To all of my patients who have allowed me to be their guide over the years…thank you for this honor.

To my friends who read and re-read early versions of this book and who have supported me in many ways, I am so very blessed to have you all in my life.

To every child, woman and man who has ever stayed silent out of fear…may my story inspire you to tell your own unique story. As we speak our stories our hearts are set free once again.

What I tell about "me" I tell about you
the walls between us long ago burned down
this voice seizing me is your voice
burning to speak to us of us.

~ Rumi

Picture Perfect

Inscrutable eyes. Glistening. Wide open. Blunt black bangs peeking out under a white hat. Ruby red lips fashioned into a broad smile. Jackie. His sheer size wrapped around her. Cheek to cheek. Bright faces framed. Baby faced. Lenny. A white corsage larger than life pinned, the promise of birth. Just married streamers waved hope from the limo bumper. Rice thrown. Confetti.

Expectation. Faith. Joy.

Snapshot of a life. Picture Perfect.

"You fucking whore." My father's voice boomed like an angry grizzly bear from the living room. I bolted from the kitchen. My tiny mother was cornered against the velvet red wall with a lump rising under her left eye. My father loomed over her, all 6'3" and 365 pounds of him. He held frozen orange juice cans in both fists.

"Dad, STOP," I screamed. He didn't flinch. He was unreachable in this white, ice-cold state of rage. "Michael!" My 14-year-old mind raced to figure out what to do.

1

Michael, my younger brother, ran down the stairs from the second floor. I ran to meet him. Brian, the baby of our family, was not far behind.

"You've got to jump him, while I get her away from him. Surprise the hell out of him!"

"You're nothing but a fucking whore. You hear me?" growled my father, baring his fangs. This father was also known by many as the funny fat man. The man with the boisterous laugh and infectious singing voice who was greeted by everyone as a long lost friend.

He was not laughing today. Without warning, this man would veer from dangerous to loving to scary. As a child it was nearly impossible to make sense of, particularly for me since I was his favorite. One moment he was filling my cheeks with warm butterfly kisses and dancing me around the room to Diana Ross, and the next he was exploding like a time bomb.

Michael jumped on my father's back, putting his head in a headlock.

"You fucking hurt her, and I will kill you. Drop the fucking cans," my brother warned. My father released his grip.

Brian grabbed the cans. I grabbed my mother, put my arm around her and walked her up to my bedroom on the third floor. She sat on the edge of my bed, lit a cigarette and took a deep drag. I flashed on the picture of my parents leaving for their honeymoon that sat in the silver frame on top of their dresser. I longed to know the woman behind the bold smile before she was erased by the flesh of his hand and demoralizing temper. Glistening eyes now deadened with fear, depression and false promises.

A dead empty silence pervaded the house. Everyone seemed to disappear. I wondered if anyone in our neighborhood knew what went on behind closed doors. Brookline was an affluent neighborhood of Boston, full of doctors, lawyers and white-collar professionals.

A Harvard educated psychiatrist who lived across the street once had us over for a Sukkot celebration, the festival of the fall harvest. Another neighbor, a rabbi, offered prayers of gratitude. As I stood smiling under their Sukkah made of various fruits and vines, I wanted to scream, "Can't you see how crazy he is?"

No. They didn't see. They couldn't see. My father was a master manipulator. He charmed everyone, perfecting our social image with fine mastery. He was the funny fat man with his smiling troupe of wife and children for all to witness.

In my bedroom, every creak of the old house sent a jolt down my body as I tended to my mother's face, while she tended to her cigarettes. My stomach tightened with each new thought of him throwing frozen orange juice cans again and again at her face as if it were a shooting target. I couldn't bear the thought of her being beaten up by him again. He beat her randomly depending upon his mood swings. I couldn't remember him not going ballistic on someone at least every few weeks. When he wasn't beating her, he beat my eldest brother Robert or me. The three of us took the brunt of his madness. I don't think my sister Jessa or my brother Brian were ever beaten.

The worst part however was the constant threat of violence that permeated the house. It was like living in a war zone. We were always on alert for the next bomb to explode.

"Mom," I said, dabbing the reddened lump under her eye with a warm washcloth, "You have to leave him."

"I can't," she said. "I have no money and nowhere to go. How could I take care of you kids? It doesn't matter anyway, Ellen. He's already told me that if I ever dare leave, he'll make sure I never see you kids again. I can't risk that." She took a hard drag on her cigarette. "I won't do that, Ellen. I won't!"

I was disgusted with her and with the whole situation. How could she stay with him, sleep in the same bed as him?

How could she keep letting him do this to her, to us?

"Mom…"

From down in the kitchen I heard a cabinet door flung open. I jumped. I was always on keen alert to my father's sounds. He coughed, grabbed something wrapped in plastic, slammed a glass on the counter and poured his nightly cup of milk. Then he stomped up to his bedroom and slammed the door. Tonight he didn't scream for her: she was safe in my room. I was grateful.

"Ellen, go to sleep. I'll be fine," she said, lighting her third Salem in a row.

"Mom…"

"Just go to sleep, Ellen. You have school in the morning. Shhh, go to sleep now."

Exhausted, I curled up under my covers with all of my clothes on. My mother curled up at the bottom of my bed and dragged on her Salem.

"No," I said, sitting up. "I'm not going to sleep. I'm sick of this and you. What are you doing?"

"Ellen," she said weakly, "haven't I had enough tonight?"

"I haven't even gotten started, and I'm not going to stop until you do something. You know what, Mom? You disgust me. I always feel so bad for you. I'm not going to feel bad anymore. You make me sick."

"E-*llen*…listen…"

"No, you listen to me. I hate you. Why are you staying here?"

Whimpering, she said, "I can't take anymore."

"And you think I can? You expect me to just sit here, be the good girl and watch you and all of us just keep getting beaten up. Why don't you do anything?"

"I can't, Ellen."

"You can, Mom. You can do anything you want, but obviously, you don't want to do anything."

"Ellen," she said, leaning towards me.

I jumped off the bed to get away from her and sat on the opposite corner of the shag rug. "I hate you," I said, crying. "Why are you doing this? I'm tired of feeling bad for you. It's always about poor you. What about us?"

"Ellen, listen to me," she said lighting up another cigarette. "I wish it were different. Don't you think I want it to be different?"

"Then make it different."

"Where am I going to get the money to support you guys?"

"Mom, you're so smart, you could do anything you want."

"And what happens every time I get a new job? He gets me fired. Do you see that?"

"But if you're not living with him, then he won't be able to run your life."

"Oh honey, I wish that were true."

"It is, Mom. It is. You just have to get away from him. Go to the police. Tell them. They can help us."

"He can convince anyone of anything. How do you think I end up in those hospitals? He can even convince a psychiatrist that I'm nuts."

"You're not nuts, Mom. You're just scared. He's just an overgrown baby. Can't you see him as a big fat overgrown gorilla who needs a big fat pacifier?" We both cracked up. I understood that my mother suffered from serious depression. I knew that the institutions he had her committed to weren't helping her. And I recognized the difference between being crazy and being depressed.

"I'm sorry, Ellen, I wish I had your spunk. You know that. I really do. I hope you never lose that. It's amazing to me. You're amazing to me. I hope you know that."

I got up, went over and gave her a big hug. "I'm so sorry, Mom. I wish I could find a way to make this better."

"It'll get better, honey. It always does. You know that. It always gets better." I crawled back into bed, lay down on my stomach and my mother caressed my upper back in the circular motion that I loved.

"Tomorrow's another day. It'll be better, I promise. Now go to sleep." She curled up at the bottom of my bed. "Sleep tight, honey."

After a few restless minutes, the room seemed too quiet. I looked at the end of my bed. My mother had already dozed off.

I tried to sleep but couldn't. My father's voice echoed in my ear: "Remember, nothing ever goes on here." He'd cornered me once as I was leaving the house, after another night of violence. I grabbed the door handle, and he put his hand over mine. "Tell me," he said.

"Nothing ever goes on here," I parroted back.

I took the cigarette out of my mother's hand, put it out in the ashtray, grabbed one of the blankets at the bottom of the bed and pulled it over her. From between the bed and wall, I pulled out my leather-bound gold-embossed journal and black pen. This was my God journal. I wrote in it almost every night.

"Dear God, I need your help. I need you to get down here and help our family. Please. I don't know what else to do."

Fear

I was 9 when I learned of my fragile start in life. I was with my Mom, my Aunt Louisa and cousins Suzanne and Robin in the car when Suzanne blurted, "Your mother left you when you were born." My stomach fell to the car floor.

"Suzanne," my aunt exclaimed.

"Mom, is it true?" I knew enough to know babies were not to be left unaccompanied.

"It wasn't exactly like that, Ellen. But it's true I couldn't take care of you." She rambled on without taking a breath, "I was sick and needed help. But Dad was there. And the nurses loved you so much. They just couldn't get over how much hair you had. Do you know how much hair you had? Bundles. They thought you were so cute. They put your hair up in a big red bow. The day you went home they wrapped you up in a big red blanket they'd bought themselves."

I was silent in the back seat. She hadn't said she loved me. Who cared if the nurses loved me? My mind was flooded by a scene of me alone in a crib without a mother to pick me up and comfort me. I picked at a scab on my leg. I must have been the cause of her nervous breakdown. I knew she didn't have any problems with the births of my other siblings. She must have hated me for making her sick. No wonder she didn't want to come home from the hospital.

And yet, an image arose in my mind of my mother holding me so tightly I could not mistake it for anything but love. I was 2, and I had taken off down the beach alone without my parents noticing. When my mother realized I was missing, she panicked. The police were notified and everyone began searching for me. The police found me and held me in the back of the police car until my mother was able to get to me. When she arrived, she grabbed me and held me as if her life depended on it.

One Saturday evening, I sat with my siblings and Dad around the kitchen table enjoying one of our ritual pizza nights. Dad took a bite of pepperoni and said, "Ellie, I'm taking you with me tomorrow to see Mom. It'll do her good to see you." I waited to see if he would mention anyone else. He didn't. I gloated, trying hard to not let it show on my face.

"Always smelly Ellie," Robert said.

My father grabbed another slice of pizza, ignoring my brother's remark. Everyone knew enough to let it go.

As we drove in our wood paneled station wagon, I couldn't sit still. I was so excited to see my mother. The bright array of the New England fall colors glimmered out the car window.

"Red, I love my bed," I blurted out. My father and I often played the color game.

"Orange, orange you glad you're my beautiful daughter." He laughed.

"Yellow, hey mister meet my father, he's a fine fellow." I giggled as my father tickled me with his right hand. With warm Indian summer air swirling around me and through my hair,

I felt special at having been chosen to go on this trip.

We took a deep right turn up a steep hill. An immaculate lawn stretched in front of us, a blue sky behind it, wide open, expectant. Dad said he'd go and get Mom. I jumped in the backseat to make room. A few moments later, he came out with a thin, drawn woman who walked towards our car with a slow shuffle like an old man. She had on everyday clothes rather than hospital clothes. Her tan pants hung off her skeletal frame. I didn't recognize the beige outer coat as anything my mother had ever owned. It was far too big and plain. It looked like it belonged to the lunch lady at school. Her rich black hair lay in oily strands plastered to her scalp. Deep purple rings outlined in a sickly yellow hue obscured her chocolate brown eyes. White pasty flesh replaced her warm olive skin. She looked like the life had been zapped out of her. Just a mere sack of a human being remained. My dad opened the passenger car door for her. She placed her left hand slowly on the seat to steady herself. Her bony arm shook. I looked at my father. He was acting as though everything was normal.

"Jack, Ellen's here to see you," he yelled, as if he were speaking to an elderly person who was hard of hearing.

She looked at me oddly with glazed eyes and said in a distant manner. "Hello."

I smiled politely.

"I'm going to go to the cafeteria and get some orange juice and give you two some time to visit. Do you want anything, Ellen?" Dad didn't wait for my answer before he slammed the car door shut.

I shoved myself against the door and tried to get the words out. Nothing came. I wanted to get out of that car and get as far away as I could from this creepy woman, but I was supposed to be nice. How could he leave me alone with her? It dawned on me that he brought me, not because I was special, but because he didn't want to deal with her. He never wanted to deal with her or her mental illness. How could I have been so stupid?

"What happened to your hair?" I managed to bark to break the unbearable silence. Her rich black hair looked like a mangy matted dogs' hair with clumps streaked with Vaseline.

She looked to see if anyone was around, pulled towards me, put nail bitten fingers by her lips and whispered: "Can I tell you a secret?"

I nodded.

"I have to get away from here. These people are mean and they want to hurt me." Her legs jerked up and down. "They put me in a padded room by myself and locked the door."

I fiddled with the doorknob.

"You're not going to tell on me, are you?" Her eyes darted. "You can't tell anyone, Okay?"

I nodded and stared out the window past the manicured lawn at the building my father had disappeared into. Why had he left me alone with this woman who hardly seemed to know who I was or that I was only 11? I thought I might vomit.

"Here, I made this for you, Ellen," she said as if saying my name for the first time. She leaned towards me. I pulled away, cringing at the thought of her touching me. "Here," she said, handing me a white trash bag.

Inside was a leather Indian beaded belt in bright colors, orange, turquoise and red.

"Do you like it? I made it in crafts class for you," she said, as if she were a child giving a parent a camp project.

"It's nice," I lied. "Thank you."

"Ellen, how are all the kids? I miss everyone."

"Everyone's fine. They miss you, too."

"I want to come home," she cried. "I wish I were coming home."

My father opened the car door. I jumped.

"Did you have a good visit?" he asked my mother, as if she

were a child. She shook her head. "Visiting time's almost over. I need to take you back."

She shot me a desperate look which went through my body like an electric shock. Her eyes screamed, "Help me."

"Dad," I began.

My mother shot another look that said, "No, that's our secret, right?"

"Are you sure Mom can't come home with us?"

"Not today, Ellie, but soon enough."

"Say goodbye to Ellen, Jack."

"Bye."

By the time my father returned to the car, I had managed to stop crying. He hated it when I cried. "Dad, can't we just bring Mom home. I don't like this place."

"She'll be coming home soon, Ellie. She needs to get well first. Okay?"

I slouched down. No matter what I did, nothing made a difference. I couldn't stop him from writing bad checks or lying. I couldn't stop him from beating my mother, my brother Robert or me. And I certainly couldn't stop him from going off into rages and having my mother committed. Our lives were spinning out of control, and there was nothing I could do.

He held up his Snickers Bar. "Wanna bite?"

"No." I covered my mouth with my right hand and held my stomach with my left.

My mother had suffered from severe depression since she was a young girl. She hardly ever admitted it. I think she must have been afraid of being put away forever. As a Jew, in her generation, the stigma against mental disorders was legendary. Parents would closet their kids away to hide mental illness. In Judaism it was not considered a sin or a punishment by God to have a psychological affliction, but many in my mother's generation acted as if it was.

The veil of secrecy surrounding mental illness only served to drive my mother's denial deeper. When her depression worsened, she'd go on drinking binges, consuming wine, vodka and gin all hours of the day and night. She'd swig straight from the bottle, as much as she could infuse into her body.

She cycled in and out of depression. Instead of therapy, she received shock treatment and heavy medications that made her act like a zombie. She told me several times she hated how the drugs made her feel. As soon as she'd feel better, she'd secretly go off of her medication cold turkey. But I could always tell; she was too happy and she barely slept.

"Mom, have you gone off your medication again?" I interrogated her one day at the kitchen table as she drank another cup of coffee.

"No Ellen, I have not."

"Mom..."

"Ellen, I swear…"

"You can't do this. Do you want to end up in the same place again? You know that's what's going to happen."

"Ellen, I swear to you, I have not gone off my medication."

"Yes you have, I can tell," I yelled at her. I put my head down on the kitchen table and sobbed. "You promised."

"Ellen, look at me." She tried to put her hand on my back. I pushed it away.

I stood up. "I hate you. You know that, I really hate you."

"Ellen…"

I ran upstairs to my bedroom. Within weeks another round of depression had begun.

My mother was brilliant. Everybody thought so. I marveled at the stack of books forever sitting next to her on the couch. She read everything from romance novels to biographies to history books. She devoured books and alcohol the way my father devoured food.

Her vocabulary and proper accent rather than the usual Bostonian drawl, combined with knowledge of history and culture, impressed everyone. She put herself through Boston University and received a teaching degree. As impressed as I was with her intelligence, I was equally confounded by her inability to reach her potential. She could've done anything she'd put her mind to. How had such a smart woman ended up in my mother's shoes? Only later did I appreciate how much my father's abuse and her mental illness undermined her self-esteem. I often prayed that God would somehow illuminate for my mother her brilliance.

I didn't have to look at my mother to know when she wasn't alright. I had learned to feel her mood, especially her anguish and fear, even at a distance.

One day, as I was walking from my bedroom half asleep toward the bathroom, I nearly tackled my dazed mother. Her matted hair looked like she had slept on it for weeks.

"Mom," I grabbed her to steady her. "What's wrong?" I'd awoken from a deep sleep, knowing in my gut something was not right with her.

"Nothing, I'm fine," she said, annoyed.

"Really?"

"Ellen, why do you always have to question me?"

"I know something's wrong. What's wrong?"

She burst into tears. "I just hate it. I hate the dreams."

"What happened?"

"I spent the night searching for Michael. He was lost, and I couldn't find him."

"It's okay."

"No, it's not okay. I spent the whole night looking for him, and I couldn't find him."

"Mom, Michael's okay. I'm sure he's in his room. Go see. He's fine." I couldn't ignore the chill that ran through my body. I knew something would happen to Michael. Her dreams had been too accurate over the years for me not to trust them.

We went downstairs to the kitchen, and she put on a pot of coffee. I was grateful she wasn't grabbing for a bottle of booze and prayed she wouldn't lose it today as she often did after a night of dreams.

Her dreams predicted the future with rare accuracy. She dreamed of people dying or conceiving children, of houses burning down and people being lost before the actual events took place. Unlike many people who today marvel at psychic gifts, my mother hated her abilities. I often wondered if she felt responsible for the information that came to her.

She'd often sit downstairs until early in the morning by herself, reading one of her many novels as a way to stave off sleep and the dreaded dreamtime. She once told me that she felt God was punishing her for something that she had done, unbeknownst to her, perhaps in a past life. The lack of sleep enhanced her emotional instability. I believe if she had been able to accept her psychic gifts, she would not have suffered from the mental instability or it would have been greatly diminished. Her mental illness was her deep psychic abilities rushing chaotically to the surface like water breaking uncontrollably through a dam.

Unlike my mother's dreams, mine were filled with adventures and comforting angels. For as long as I could remember, I had nightly visits with angel friends.

I'd drift off to sleep under a mountainous heap of worn blankets and awaken as I was flying out my bedroom window where I was greeted by seven angels. Although they were not clear in form, I could see them. They appeared as various shades of lights, ranging from pink to blue. Different personalities emanated from them. Some seemed older and wiser, as if they were the big brothers and sisters.

We communicated via group thought like birds. We flew

from place to place helping kids in need all over the world, in their homes, on playgrounds and in hospitals.

One evening, a thought was passed between us suggesting we go visit a children's hospital ward. In the same moment we were transported to the ward. We stood at the foot of a bed with a young boy named Bruce, who was no older than 12. He had a white bandage wrapped around the left side of his shaven head. He smiled, knowing we were there. The nurses didn't seem to notice us. The eldest of the group spoke to Bruce telepathically, "What can we do for you?"

"Can you help my parents not to worry so much? It hurts to feel the pain they think they're hiding from me."

"We'll work with them as much as we can but they must feel their pain. It's their journey. And you must allow yourself to feel your own pain and feelings, not theirs. It will be better this way."

"Is there anything I can do for them?" Bruce asked, with the saddest blue eyes I had ever seen.

"Feel your own joy. You have a lot of joy to share with the world."

At first, I couldn't see Bruce's joy, but as the angel spoke, I began to feel it emanating from the boy. I saw a pink light arising from his heart area, and he seemed to be enveloped in blue and purple. His blues eyes began to shine. I was being shown how to see beyond how most of us usually see. We were meeting Bruce outside the bounds of time and words. Light meeting light, light bodies expanding into one another.

We helped children in hospitals, orphanages, wards of various kinds, as well as children in despair. We did funny things to make them laugh. One of my angel friends loved to dance his light around the room. It was a spectacular light show that always made the kids laugh.

Although my travels with my celestial friends took place in the dreamtime and astral space, I knew they were real. More real than anything I could explain. I became brutally aware that others, especially my father, did not agree with my assessment. The one and only time I told him about my spirit friends, he warned me to never speak with such stupidity. I learned to keep my flying adventures and angelic companions to myself.

But I felt a great need to share the lessons of this other realm. There I learned what so many spiritual teachers throughout time have professed, a truth of love and spirit beyond our daily reality. I learned universal truths that outweighed the skepticism of our increasingly violent and destructive world. Through their understanding, I learned that none of us are alone. We all have guides and angels working with us, waiting to be asked for help. They are able to see beyond our wrongs to our hearts. These angelic companions taught me that love is a universal truth that we all yearn to learn. Love is our main reason for incarnating and having an earthly experience.

Years later, I told the story of my celestial entourage and some of what I had learned to a grieving parent as we sat with her child who lay dying of cancer. "I want you to know," I said, "no matter what it may look like to you right now, you and your daughter will never be separated, even in her death. And she will not be alone. She, like all of us, has guides and angels looking out for her." The grieving mother's eyes filled with deep gratitude. My heart was forever changed.

I was amazed that I had risked sharing my story. I had held this knowledge to myself for years, never willing to risk being humiliated. It wasn't just my father who didn't believe in angels or guides. What seemed ordinary to me was considered fantasy by many. And yet I knew beyond a shadow of doubt that without my angels and guides, I never would have endured my chaotic and violent childhood.

Still, even after I learned the truth of love and spiritual support, I struggled with the concept of a loving God. How could a loving God put a child in the path of a violent father like mine? How could a loving God allow women to be raped, wars to be fought and people to be killed? Was God or anyone listening? I couldn't see my prayers being answered.

It was only with enough time, years later, that I recognized that my guides were indeed watching over me. I learned they are always with me, with all of us. I also learned that they must allow us – me, my father, my mother, everyone – to have free will. Otherwise, we'd just be puppets on a celestial string.

I worked with the angelic cohorts until I was 12. As I was coming back through my window, which was used as both the entry and departure point, I was told that I had to have a meeting with the Board.

I was transported to a meeting room enclosed by glass. Six people were seated at a table that took up most of the space.

"You have served with us very well," a distinguished man with a prominent shock of white hair stated, "but it's time for you to make an important decision. You must decide if you wish to continue your journey with us or continue your journey with your parents."

I understood the choice. Staying with them would mean my earth body would die. Even though life was difficult with my parents, I knew I needed to remain with them. The decision made, my heart pounded. Never again would I see the celestial light beings. My heart ached. The angelic cohort surrounded me with their enormous love. "Know that we are always with you." My heart filled with their warm love flowing through it.

In the next instant, I sailed back in through my window and landed in my bed. I never flew with them again.

For years, I begged my father for one of the empty bedrooms on the third floor. He denied every request. He never had a good reason. I desperately wanted my own bedroom. My little sister Jessa and I shared a room with green wallpaper splashed with delicate red flowers, but I wanted a place where I could think alone, write and smoke cigarettes without getting caught.

One day in early spring while my family was out, I decided to lay claim to a third floor bedroom. I carried my box spring and mattress up the steep staircase on my back. Next came the solid wood dresser. I took the drawers out. It was longer than I was tall and weighed as much as I did. Pulling and pushing it to the edge of the staircase, I got up on the first step, crept down, got into position and hoisted the dresser upon my back. After the first two steps, I realized it would have to be maneuvered into a steep curve in the staircase. I imagined what I looked like and began to laugh so hard I was afraid I would pee my pants or drop the dresser and shatter it to pieces. My stomach muscles ached. A vivid image shot through my mind of Sherpas and donkeys in Nepal carrying heavy loads. I imagined myself as a little Sherpa boy in Nepal. Somehow using this imagery, and leaning against the wall for support, I found the strength to hoist the dresser one more time into a position up higher on my back to make it through the difficult curve. Four more steep steps and I lowered the dresser onto the landing, balanced it against the wall and crouched down in laughter. I couldn't believe my own strength.

Not knowing when my father would return, I forced myself to hustle without taking a break to get the room furnished and completed. I knew if I could do this, I'd win the bedroom. I ran up and down the stairs, grabbing the dresser drawers, taking the thick white shag rug from the attic, putting the box spring and mattress on top of the rug. The rug had an uncanny resemblance to our white Samoyed dog, Eerie.

Within an hour, I had created a safe nest in my otherwise crazy household. There, I'd be free to have my own opinion about everything, dream about my life beyond our house, scream back at my father, protect my mother, speak to God and dream with my angel friends.

I grabbed the hairbrush off my dresser and turned and looked straight into the mirror. I sang one of my father's favorite songs, "Aint no mountain high enough." For once, I wasn't self-conscious about my voice. I felt free to be the singer I could only dream about. I forgot that I thought I had a horrible voice. With abandon, I bowed to my imaginary audience and cracked myself up, laughing so hard I snorted. I secretly loved having an audience and being a star.

I sat on my bed, stared out the window and thought of my father's singing voice. He was the real singer of the family. He could've been famous. People who heard him often said so. I wished he could have heard his own voice, operatic, deep, sonorous. Instead, I suspected he only heard Nannie's voice, telling him how horrible he was.

I often thought about what my parents could have been. My mother, with her intelligence and love for the literary arts, would've been a great writer. If only they'd had their own voices to create a life they were happy with. I wonder if they could've nurtured me then.

I heard my parents arriving home and ran downstairs.

"Dad, I have something to show you. Come upstairs."

Today I knew it was safe to play. Even though things change in an instant, I had gotten pretty good at feeling out his moods.

"Right now?"

"Yes, I have to show you something."

"Ellen, what on earth did you do now?"

I laughed. "You'll see."

As we got to the landing, I jumped to open my new bedroom door. "Ta-da."

His eyes lit up, and he cracked up laughing. "My, oh my. Jack," he yelled to my mother. "Come upstairs."

"You're something else, aren't you?" He grabbed me and gave me a big hug. "Alright, you got me. You won it fair and square," he said, laughing. I raised my arms up in victory and did a celebratory dance.

"How the hell did you get this up here?" he asked, pointing at the dresser.

Just then my mother arrived. "Oh, for goodness sake, Ellen. How did you get all of this up here?"

"I carried it up on my back."

"On your back?" My parents said in unison, in disbelief. It was fun to see my parents getting along and laughing together.

My father laughed so hard I thought he might pee his pants. My mother shook her head.

"It looks beautiful, Ellen. You have a way with things just like your father. You certainly didn't get it from me."

"Just one thing," my father said. "You can't sit out on the perch. Promise me you won't sit out there." The perch was a decorative architectural roof feature used in the 1900's when the house was built. It extended out from under the diamond-shaped paned windows. It was never intended to be sat upon.

"I promise." I crossed my fingers behind my back, knowing the perch was the exact reason I had chosen this bedroom over the larger bedroom on the third floor.

He squeezed me tighter and gave me a kiss on my forehead. "Ellie, you earned it."

Within a few months, the tension in the house had gotten considerably worse. Bad days outnumbered good ones. My father's moods became darker and lasted longer. Money had gotten tighter. My father told me about a business deal that had fallen through.

"It was a big one, Ellie," he said, sitting at his desk in the living room flipping through his leather bound phone book with the broken spine.

"Does it have any hope?"

"I think she's dead in the water. But you know me; there will be another deal just around the next corner. Right?"

"Right," I said smiling.

The next day he took me with him to the electric company. He spoke to a woman named Mary behind the counter. She laughed every few sentences and threw her blonde hair back. After a few minutes, he convinced her to keep our electricity on, promising her he'd have money for her in a few days. "As soon as the check arrives, I'll get you paid up. Thank you, Mary." I smiled at the woman, and knew he was lying. He was always waiting for another check to arrive.

Faith

"Sh'ma Yisrael Adonai Eloheinu, Adonai Echad." The words flowed through me this Friday evening like a steady stream. "Adonai Eloheinu, Adonai Echad," I sang louder as I dressed in my favorite black and white plaid skirt and white cashmere mock turtleneck sweater that I wore only to Temple. I imagined all the women at Temple in their stylish outfits and sparkly jewelry winking and nodding at me with approval.

Hopping up on my bed to look at myself in the mirror, I fussed with my fine brown hair and sang, "Sh'ma Yisrael" to my Jewish women ancestors as I imagined dark round women huddled behind and beside me, whispering and guiding me on properly preparing for Temple. Their soft words of wisdom reminded me of the saying from the Talmud, *Every blade of grass has its angel that bends over it and whispers, "Grow, grow."* Tonight, I was my ancestor's little sprout. Even without my mother, I was not alone. With their guidance, I managed to get my slippery fine hair pulled up away from my face with a bit of my hair left down in the back for a most pleasing contrast.

I bent my knees and mimicked how my father admired himself in the mirror when he bought new clothes, straight on, sideways and from the back. "Yes," I whispered. I put on the special gold ring with my initials engraved on it that my father gave me for Hanukah.

"Ellen, let's go," my father yelled from downstairs. "Come on. Let's go. Now."

Sneaking one last peak in the mirror, I hopped off the bed and ran downstairs and out the front door into our new wood-paneled station wagon. Under my father's patrol, all five of us kids got out of the house on schedule. My mother trailed behind like a dark shadow.

"Get out," my brother Robert yelled, "That's my seat. Out!"

"Ouch," I squealed, "let me…"

"Knock it off. I swear…knock it off," my father warned.

I pinched my brother and shot him a stern look. He blasted me a nasty gaze back. We knew better than to continue to fight out loud.

"Let's play the Be Quiet game," my father said.

We all closed our mouths at once. Robert turned and made a face. I stuck my fingers in my nose and pulled my nostrils toward my forehead. As we pulled up to a red light, Michael upped the ante by making mean faces and mouthing fatherly words as he pointed at us behind Dad's head. I couldn't help it; I cracked up and lost the game. I didn't care. I was too excited to get to Temple. It was one of the few places I felt safe.

I spent hours thinking about religions and God. I didn't just go to Temple, but also went church hopping every few weeks with my friends. My favorite was Dixie's Roman Catholic Church. The old Latin prayers and Gregorian chants put me in a trance. I loved learning about their rituals and music and was determined to understand all the diverse ways people spoke to and glorified God all over the world. It confused and saddened me, though, how people fought and killed each other in the name of God, certain this was not what God had intended.

As we drove up Harvard Street, the Temple sat in the middle of an old tree-lined street. The original stone building was built in 1928, and the congregation had an even older history, having begun as Congregation Israel in 1854 by German members of Temple Chabel Shalom. I often imagined these German members sitting amongst us whispering their ideals. These founding members held an important vision. From the very beginning, they encouraged and supported women and people from all faiths to be active in their community. I was proud these were my people.

To reach the four large columns of its grand entrance, you had to climb fifty-two narrow steps. Between the columns were two oversized, wrought-iron doors. I never understood why the doors were so enormous and heavy, but thankfully they were always open when we arrived.

Unlike some of the churches I went to, the Temple ceilings were high but not arched. The main hall was an open room lit with candlelight and warm lighting. The wood floor was lined with light maple benches cushioned in purple velvet, which faced the Rabbi's pulpit, the Cantor's high backed chair and the Ark, which held the blessed Torah.

After saying hello to people from the congregation, being kissed and having my cheeks squeezed too hard by the older women, we took our seats close to the pulpit on the left-hand side. The seven of us took up almost the entire row. I loved sitting close to the Rabbi's pulpit and the Ark.

"Welcome, Shabbat Shalom," the Rabbi said.

"Shabbat Shalom," the congregation replied in unison.

"First, before we begin tonight, I'd like to take care of Temple business. I'd like to thank the Hadassah women's group for raising $1,000 for the kids' summer program."

Robert and I flapped our arms like chickens. It was our code for the old Hadassah women whose sagging arm skin gave us the willies. My father shot us a look. We stopped. I turned so my back was toward him. Hand over my mouth, I tilted my head back and pretended a good long yawn. My brother grinned.

After what felt like an eternity, the Rabbi began the service. I sat up straight and listened. He talked about love, not a romantic love but a neighborly love. "On this Shabbat," he said, "each one of us are called upon as children of Egypt to reach and extend ourselves out to those in need of love, comfort and support."

"Sh'ma Yisrael, Sh'ma Eloheinu, Sh'ma Echad," sang the Cantor in his deep, sonorous voice, leading the congregation in what is considered the most important prayer of Judaism. Michael turned his lips over his teeth as though he were an old man and whispered, "Sh'ma," and then pretended to die. I nearly laughed out loud but managed to cough instead. My father shot us a look that said, "Cut it out or else."

In unison, the congregation answered the Cantor, "Sh'ma Yisrael, Adonai Eloheinu, Adonai Echad," in a slow melody, elongating each vowel. The sounds enveloped me like a warm fuzzy blanket.

We read a few prayers in Hebrew from our prayer book while I impatiently awaited the opening of the Ark. It was made of a light maple and stood seven feet tall and was placed against the back wall.

Finally, the Rabbi walked to the Ark and opened its intricately carved doors. Inside, the Torah stood upright in a dark plum velvet covering. With reverence, the Rabbi lifted it from the Ark. The Cantor standing beside him removed the ornamental breast plate and mantel to reveal the scrolls. The Rabbi gently placed the sacred scrolls onto the narrow shoulders of

13-year-old Mark Bloom. Mark was honored to carry the Torah as part of his Bar Mitzvah preparation.

Together, Mark, the Rabbi and Mark's father walked shoulder to shoulder carrying the Torah through the Temple, allowing the congregation to receive its blessings. My stomach flipped and flopped. Robert had told me that if someone dropped the Torah, even if by accident, they would have to die. I held my breath, afraid that skinny Mark with way too many pimples would drop the Torah and have to die. As it passed me, I kissed my fingers and shot my hand out to bless it, praying I wouldn't unsteady Mark. When the scrolls were brought back to the Rabbi's pulpit and laid down, I breathed a deep sigh of relief.

Like most Torahs, ours had traveled the world, coming from Poland and somehow managing to survive the Holocaust. The text was handwritten in ancient Hebrew calligraphy which didn't look at all like letters to me, rather more like the beautiful swirls and squiggles I spent hours drawing in my journals. I thought it would be great to have the Hebrew letters painted all over my body, like the abstract designs women tattooed on their bodies in ancient Egypt.

While the Rabbi read from the sacred text in early Hebrew, I thought about all the others who had come before me and kissed our Torah, all those who had listened to this very same reading. What did they look like? Did they have brown hair and hazel brown eyes like me? Or did they look different? All these different Jewish people lived in different places, in Poland, Germany, Russia, Spain, Israel, Africa and even China. And yet we were all Jewish. Jewish girls, so different, yet all the same.

When I was born, my father thought I looked Chinese with my jet-black hair, jaundiced skin and squinty eyes. If I could have talked then, I would have said, "You should see the Jews who live in China. Don't worry."

I was thrilled to realize there were Jewish girls all over the world who looked like me and many who looked just like my Christian friends with blond hair and blue eyes, and still others who had black hair and blue eyes. Bubbling over with excitement, I leaned toward my father and whispered, "Dad, we're all the same."

He shot me a disapproving glare.

I rolled my eyes, knowing he didn't get it. Had he heard a word the Rabbi had said?

Just a few weeks earlier my family was driving down Boylston Street on our way to Chinatown for dinner. My dad spotted a young black man and a white woman walking arm in arm, giggling.

"Would you look at that, Jack, in broad daylight no less."

From the back seat I blurted, "They look happy together, isn't that what matters?" As soon as the words flew out of my mouth I knew I was in trouble. I should have known better than to say anything, but his racist comments infuriated me. I knew it didn't matter what your skin color was.

"I didn't hear anyone asking you, Ellen, did I?" he said as he sped up the car. My father pulled into the parking space too quickly. We all piled out of the car. As I walked closer to my father, he grabbed my arm. Squeezing the flesh between his fat, stubby fingers and palm, the blood coursed into my fingertips. I held my breath and tightened my body, trying not to show it. Yanking my face close to his, his blood shot eyes bulged as he said, "No daughter of mine will ever be a nigger lover. Am I making myself clear?"

I bowed my head and nodded. With a shove, he released his grip on me.

Tonight, in Temple, our Rabbi was saying what I knew to be true, we should love everyone. Would he include my father if he knew what he did? He didn't say love everyone except for people who were mean or who had dark skin, no money and a poor education. No, he said love everyone. I took his words to heart and wondered if my father ever would.

Even with his disapproving eyes, racist thoughts and beatings, I took it upon myself to love my father. He wasn't always cruel. For these few hours at Temple, he was the kind, loving, jovial even reverent man everyone loved. In these moments, I was proud to be his daughter. Together we recited prayers, sang songs of praise for life and God. Together we were united. We were whole and happy at least for a few hours.

The Rabbi put the Torah back in the Ark. We stood and bowed our heads as we remembered all those who had come before us. In unison, the men dipped their knees and bowed their heads as they recited the Kaddish (the prayer for the dead) in deep monotone voices to a haunting staccato beat. They looked like waves moving along the ocean shore.

Here within the Temple walls, I was not alone. It didn't matter that my father didn't understand me. Even the thought of my mother's vacant eyes hurt less. I took a deep breath and felt my women ancestors huddled and praying with me.

Y'he sh'meh rabba m'varakh
L' 'alam ul 'al 'me 'al 'maya
Yitbarakh v'yishtabbach v'yitpa 'ar V'yitromam
V'yitnasse v'yihaddar v'yit 'alle V'yithallal
Sh'meh d'qudsha, b'rikh hu.
L' 'ella (l 'eela mikkol) min kol birkhata
V'shirata tushb'chata v'nechemata
Da 'amiran b'alma v'imru amen
Titqabbal tz'lot'hon uva 'ut'hon
D'khol bet ysra'el
Qodam avuhon di bishmaya
V' imru amen.

May His great name be blessed.
Forever and to all eternity.
Blessed and praised, glorified and exalted,
Extolled and honored, elevated and lauded,
Be the Name of the Holy One, blessed be he.

Mother

I ran into the kitchen where my mother was cooking. "Mom, look I found a picture of me when I was a baby." By the time I was nine, most of my baby pictures had been lost in two floods. Each time I found one, it was like finding a buried treasure.

She glanced at the black and white photo. "Oh honey, no, that's my baby picture." She pointed to her outfit. "My grand-mother, your great-grandmother, knitted that for me."

My heart fell. It was easy to understand my confusion. I was the spitting image of her in a more petite package. Happy to look like her, I was terrified of ever becoming like her. Even though she didn't like dressing up or doing her makeup, I thought her face was as pretty as any movie star. And when she did dress up, she turned heads.

My mother had a feminine curvy body, but she was mas-culine in how she approached herself. She didn't spend time on picking out clothing. I'm not sure she had an aesthetic bone in her body. She'd throw on whatever happened to be closest in her closet or drawer. She had no real interest in hair, makeup or having her fingernails painted. If she ever had them done, it was at the behest of my father or because I did them for her. Left on her own, she would have been happiest in a pair of jeans, a T-shirt, a basic pair of shoes, and a short, no fuss haircut that she could shake when she woke and be done with it. Looking good was not important to her.

She tended to her hair the same way she folded laundry. She seemed to do all the right steps. Fold the corners to meet, part her hair correctly on the side. Still, the laundry ended up in a balled-up heap in the laundry basket. Her hair ended up looking like a bird's nest on top of her head. Left alone, she was quite attractive, thick jet-black hair and blunt short bangs, outlining almond shaped brown eyes. With eye lashes long enough to sweep up any man and a broad ruby smile, she was a catch. She never knew it.

She kept her hair on the shorter side. When it grew long she looked like a straggly Afghan dog, her face hidden by all the hair. Something that was never hidden, though, were her obscenely large breasts. I prayed I wouldn't inherit them. She never had a good word to say about them, from sweaters that would not fit, to feeling odd as she grew up. They were not a problem for my father. He loved them. He'd look at me as I was developing and say, "It's a shame you didn't get your mother's breasts, a damn shame." I'd fold my arms over my chest, roll my eyes and walk away. But that didn't stop him. He talked about everyone's breasts, mine, my mother's, my girlfriends'.

Unlike my mother, my father was obsessed with appearance, hers, his, and ours. For an obese man, it was odd that he was so fixated on looks. You'd think it would have stopped him from consuming nightly bags of Nestle Crunch bars, M&M's and Mars Mound bars, but it never did.

"Jack, Jack, where are you? You ready to go?" my father yelled as we entered the house after a trip to the supermarket.

My mother wandered down the stairs in her baby blue nightgown looking half asleep. I wanted to say, "Mom, you knew you were supposed to be ready by the time we got back from the store. Why aren't you ready?"

My father beat me to it. His faced turned beet red. "Oh for Christ sakes, Jack. How is it that you're not ready? What's wrong with you? The least you could have done was get ready. What the fuck were you doing all this time? Get ready. Now!"

Mom didn't say a word, she just turned with her head down and scuttled back up the stairs to get ready. I wanted to run after her, scream at her to fight back. I wanted to go back to the market with my nice Dad. I wanted to be anywhere but standing there. As I tried to creep away, his booming voice caught me. "Ellen, finish putting that stuff away."

He pounded up the stairs like a hungry grizzly bear ready for the kill. I prayed that my mother was ready by the time he got up to the bedroom. I wanted to run up and sing Diana Ross's songs to distract him. But nothing could deter him. I waited and listened intently. The silence scared me.

Within minutes, my father yelled, "Ellen, let's go." I threw the lettuce in the fridge and scurried to the front door. My brothers and sister got to stay home and watch TV. I slid in the back seat. My mother sat in the front seat. Not one word was uttered as we drove.

As we turned the corner onto Washington Avenue, my father said, "Make sure you tell them not to make it too high on the top." My mother nodded. The car came to an abrupt halt in front of Sally's Beauty Shop. She got out.

"We'll pick you up in an hour. Be ready in an hour," he said as he sped off.

I slid forward, put my hand out to stop myself from crashing into the back of his seat. He turned on the radio. I fiddled with the doorknob, turning it round and round and stared out the window. It was a bright sunny day. The glare made the road look like an ice skating rink. Melting snow dripped from roof tops, cars and sidewalks. Spring had come early and swiftly. I wanted to be outside jumping on the last of the snow piles and sloshing in the puddles.

"You hungry?" my father asked.

I jumped. "I don't know."

He made a U-turn. "Wanna go to Hidleman's and get a bite to eat?" It wasn't a real question as he was already driving there.

"Okay." Anything would have been better than sitting in this heavy, silent air.

Hidleman's was a German pastry shop filled with cinnamon strudel, honey buns, donuts, my father's favorite apple turnover that oozed of gooey chunks of apple, pies, chocolate and vanilla cakes, wedding cakes, two different soups for lunch, diamond-shaped cucumber and cheese sandwiches that looked naked without their crust and old German women scurrying behind the counter who spoke so loudly their spit flew through the air. Dad got his apple turnover, a cinnamon strudel, and a hot chocolate to share. I got a chocolate donut with jimmies. I took a sip of the chocolate, thought about my mom and felt nauseous. I didn't take another sip.

Afterwards, we ran an errand at M&K's hardware shop. My father got keys made while I walked up and down the aisles breathing in the rubbery smell and touching everything: nails, hammers, a shovel with sharp jagged teeth, a screw driver, a green garden hose, yellow rubber gloves, a bag of dirt.

"Come on, Ellie. Let's go get your mother."

We drove two blocks on Washington Avenue. I spied Mom coming out of the beauty shop. Her hair looked perfect. She'd smell of hairspray, and I couldn't wait to touch her shellacked hair.

As she got in the car, Dad screamed, "Didn't I tell you, didn't I tell you…" He pulled away from the curb and made a sharp right onto View Street. He hated when they teased her hair up into a high bouffant. "Look at you. For God's sake, look at you. Didn't I tell you to tell them not to do it like that? Look at you, for God's sake." He slapped her across the face with the back of his hand. I pushed back against the seat and squeezed my fingers together. He jammed on the brakes.

"Go," he screamed. "Make them fix it right now. Go. Get out of here."

I wondered if she liked her new hairdo. It was her hair. I thought it looked good. She was so pretty it didn't matter. And it didn't matter to her. She was never interested in things like that. She liked books and...what else? Did she like anything else? Did she have things that she liked in secret?

I often dreamt my mother had a secret life where she could do anything she wanted to without having to worry about being screamed at by my father. I'd fantasize that one day, when my father was at a business meeting, she'd grab us, have a getaway car waiting and take us away. She could wear her hair anyway she liked and stay in her bathrobe all day if she wanted to.

As she walked back into the beauty parlor, head bowed, I prayed that something would calm him down, or to be released from the prison of the back seat. I moved closer to the door, my fingers hugging the handle.

"You're not going anywhere. Don't even think of it," he said. I didn't dare move. Would the beauty parlor ladies see the redness of my mom's cheek? Would they look away? Did she cry on their shoulders, or did they just fix her hair? Time passed. Too much time passed. Dad barreled out of the station wagon and bolted into the beauty parlor. He dragged her out by the arm.

We drove home in a threatening silence. The car came to an abrupt halt in front of our house.

"Get in there and get dressed. Put on those black pleated pants," he demanded.

She walked in the house as though in a trance. She never looked back at me.

"Ellen, get in there and clean up the kitchen," he screamed.

"Madame, welcome to Chez Ellen. Please come in," I said, opening the bathroom door. "What shall we do today?"

Every few weeks, my mother would come to my make-believe beauty salon located in the upstairs bathroom. She'd shower and wash her hair to prepare herself for the makeover.

"The usual will be just fine," she said.

"Wonderful, a blow dry and makeup, yes?"

"Yes."

"Please have a seat." She sat on the toilet cover. "Let's first do the blow dry, then the makeup." I weeded my fingers through her wet hair.

"That will be wonderful."

I could feel my mother's breath deepen and her body relax as I blew dried her hair. When I finished, I took a warm washcloth and draped it over her face.

"Oh, that feels so good," she said, sinking deeper into her seat.

"And I haven't even gotten to the best part." I lathered her petite face with a heavy crème moisturizer I found in the cabinet drawer. Her olive skin made her look like she had a tan like the movie stars, and it accentuated her brown eyes and broad smile.

"You have magic hands, Ellen. I don't know where you got them from but they are magical."

"Thank you," I said, massaging her face. I applied her makeup with great seriousness. She made funny faces as the brush bristles tickled her skin. "Madame, you must try and sit still."

"Oh, yes, of course," she said, repositioning herself, sitting taller.

Her composure only lasted a few seconds before the next round of funny faces. We both cracked up. Once I finished, she got up and looked in the mirror.

"Oh that's beautiful, Ellen, just beautiful. I don't know how you do it."

"It's simple, you just…"

"No, you just have that special touch. You make me beautiful."

She was my mom. I wanted her to be beautiful. I wanted her to care about how she looked for herself and me. And most importantly, I wanted her to care about life. If she cared about life and herself, she'd be a role model. I'd have a mom. She'd show me how to be a woman. I wouldn't grow up wondering what secrets all other women knew. I'd feel like I belonged.

"It's because you're beautiful, Mom."

"Your Dad will be proud of you. He'll love it."

Once, when I was four, I sat at the kitchen table and insisted she paint my nails. As she dabbed the red liquid on my tiny nails, she said, "Where did you come from? You are so different than me."

As I got older, I kept her comment close to my heart. I was certain to name all the ways in which we were different. This cataloging served as a kind of health insurance against ever getting her disease. I promised myself I would never allow anyone to treat me the way my father treated her. My mantra: No man will ever put his hands on me.

One evening, I heard them fighting downstairs in their bedroom. The next thing I knew, my mother was sitting at the bottom of my bed, smoking a cigarette. This happened about once or twice a week. She'd escape from my dad to my bedroom very close to my bedtime and curl up at the bottom of my bed and drag on a Salem. These were some of my favorite moments alone with her.

It was the perfect opportunity to ask her questions about

her life. I was hungry to know more about her parents and what she was like as a kid. She never wanted to talk about her life. Every once in a while she'd tell me something that I would file away under the heading, "Mother's Life," so I could remember to ask more questions later to build my story about who she was.

"Mom, what were your parents like?"

"My father was very smart. He was a lawyer."

"So maybe that's how you got to be so smart."

"Probably."

"And what was your mom like."

"She was very different than me."

"Really? Like how?"

"I don't know, but I do know it's time for you to go to sleep."

That was the end of the Million Questions Game for that day. She didn't like telling elaborate stories like me.

"What about a story."

"Ellen, you know I…"

"Please, a short one."

"Okay," she said with a sigh, "once upon a time…"

"No a real story, please."

"Ellen, you tell it."

"Okay. It was a dark cold evening. The wind was just beginning to round up the mountain. Inside the old cabin by the river, you could hear the wind beginning to take hold. Cre—ak, ur, cre—ak. The old man who lived there for forever had let his grandson come and visit during his Christmas break. The boy now awakened by the wind lay in his bed too afraid to move. Suddenly he heard a strange, louder sound…"

It seemed too quiet. At the end of the bed, my mother had fallen asleep. I sat up, bent forward, took the cigarette dangling from her mouth and stamped it out in the ashtray. I grabbed a blanket, pulled it over her. Shouldn't I be the one to fall asleep first? I wanted to be the one tucked in by my mother. I wanted to be the kid, not the mom.

Over the years, I glued my mother's answers together like a puzzle. I concluded that she had suffered from depression from an early age. She told me on one of her late night visits to my bedroom that she could remember waking up as a young girl crying for no apparent reason. It was difficult to know if it was something she was born with or if it was a consequence of her family life. Her father, who was her hero, died from a brain tumor when she was eight. She was not permitted to attend his funeral. Her mother cried for days, wishing out loud she had died with her husband. A week later, her mother announced that she would have to go to work full time. My mother was left to be taken care of by her German grandmother. I never knew this grandmother's name, just that she was the tough German grandmother. I had images of her doing strange things to my mother: giving her enemas, scrubbing her clean in the bathtub with something like Ajax or lye. I didn't know where they came from, but they felt so real that I must have overheard them. I had an awful habit of listening in on my parents' conversations between themselves, their friends and our relatives.

"Yes," my mother said when I told her I suspected her grandmother was truly abusive to her. "I believe you are right."

Strangely though, my mother once called me to tell me that her cousin Sandy had found a tablecloth that had belonged to her grandmother. She was elated. Her reaction stunned me. I would never have wanted anything from her. I would have torched the tablecloth with delight.

My mother had plenty of external reasons to be depressed. Yet, she felt there was something terribly wrong with her rather than something wrong with how she was dealt with. Had she been allowed to grieve her father's death, had she not lost her mother to an abusive grandmother, had her father lived until she had grown up, had she not ended up with my father, perhaps she never would have had depression. Perhaps her self-esteem would have remained intact and she would have loved to play my Million Dollar Question game. And I would have grown up knowing my mother.

On a typical day my mom and dad awoke later than me. Wide awake without an alarm clock, I treasured the quiet of the house and my time alone to daydream before I had to shower and get dressed for school.

Once dressed, I'd walk down to my parent's bedroom, give my Dad a kiss good morning and get lunch money out of one of his pant pockets. My mom was usually still asleep or dozing off and on. Some days he'd ask me to make sure the kids had lunch money and breakfast.

My parents didn't have regular jobs. Mom had a teaching degree from Boston University and loved to teach, but Dad always managed to get her fired. He'd show up, demanding she be paid more and threaten the school. All it took was one of his visits, and she'd get fired. The last time Mom got fired she worked as an assistant teacher at an elementary school near our house when I was 13. She must have gotten tired of his antics because she stopped looking for work.

Mom spent a great deal of time on the crushed blue sofa in the den reading books or sleeping. She read everything from trashy romance novels to historical books. Often when I came home from school, she'd be sleeping on the couch in her flared blue jeans and a crumpled cotton blouse. There was always a stack of books piled beside the couch waiting to be read and an overflowing basket of laundry waiting to be folded.

She'd say she was just resting her eyes but her hair looked matted down on one side the way she looked when she got out of bed. The only hint that she hadn't slept all day was that she reeked of coffee and cigarettes.

On a good day, I think she read, watched a few soap operas, did as little housekeeping as possible without setting off my father's alarm bells and got dinner together. She loved soaps. My first name was chosen based on a character on As the World Turns.

As Mom's depression worsened, she'd drink to numb her pain. I would inevitably pick up the slack by doing the laundry, the dishes, cooking dinner, helping out with the kids and keeping my dad from exploding. I became the second mom to both my siblings and my parents. I once found a picture of me and my mom. We were sitting on the couch in the living room. You could see the depression in her eyes, drawn face, and slumped body. I was shocked to see that I looked just as exhausted and depressed.

Part of what frustrated and exhausted me was that neither parent would admit when my mother was going into one of her downward spirals. Rather than seek help, my father would scream or hit her. His favorite thing to say to her was, "You need to snap out of this, Jackie." Even I could see this was not something you just snapped out of.

I stored a series of snap shots of my mother in my mind. Through the pictures, I created a story. Over time, the pictures collapsed into a kaleidoscope. Many were of the ugly, mad, depressed mother. The worst pictures were of the faraway, absent mother, the mother I could not reach. I often imagined she and I were like two pretty party dresses hanging from an empty clothesline, side by side, flapping in whatever direction the wind happened to blow us. Waiting expectantly to be chosen for the next dance.

Even though I was afraid of my mother and her disease, I longed to be close to her. Yet, when she would try and be close to me, I withdrew. Her impulses to be affectionate made my stomach stir.

She never greeted me with the kind of enthusiasm Janie's

mom greeted Janie and me after school. I would have given anything for my mom to be like Janie's mom. Janie's mom had warm cookies and hot chocolate waiting for us. The house was immaculately clean and everything was in its place. Janie's house was perfect and calm. It looked like it belonged in *Good Housekeeping*. Unlike Janie's Mom, my mom didn't have a life of her own.

It was difficult for me to find the real woman beneath the scared, scarred woman who was so beaten down. One of the things that always remained, however, was my mother's sense of humor. She could find a way to laugh through the ridiculous situations she found herself in. And she always held on to hope. I once asked her how she got through all of it, and she said, "I just knew one day it would get better." Beneath her war scars as a captive prisoner, my mother was quite humane. She cared about animals and people who had been treated poorly or judged badly. She had a soft spot for the underdogs of the world.

There were moments, though, when I experienced her rage for the feminine and me. As a budding teen, my body went through a difficult stage. I went from being a lithe little girl who had been nicknamed Gumby (for my flexibility and small size in gymnastics) to feeling like a 400 pound gorilla. Nothing fit. I outgrew all my favorite clothes. I had breasts that hurt, and I didn't understand how to deal with them. Going shopping was a nightmare. I had hysterical tantrums in department stores that my father could not understand. To try and reason with me, he'd scream at me. It never helped. I don't know if most girls would have talked to their moms, but I didn't talk to mine. I didn't talk to anyone about how horrible I was feeling about myself and my body.

One day, my mother walked into my bedroom wearing one of my favorite pair of hot pants. "I think they look better on me than on you. Don't you think so?"

Everything in me felt white cold. I couldn't speak, could barely breathe. My stomach ached as though someone had socked me hard in the gut. Tears of distrust, betrayal and rage filled my eyes. After a few moments, she turned and left the room. Nothing more was ever mentioned about my hot pants.

The only two things I ever remember doing alone with my Mom occurred when I was 14. I arranged and brought her to see a Broadway show for her birthday. I don't remember what play we saw, but I know she liked it. The second event was later that spring. She brought me to a workshop on our bodies and sexuality.

It was hard to imagine my mother as a feminist, but she felt she was. To show her allegiance to the Women's Movement and equal rights for women, she stopped wearing a bra despite being a 36 double E. Her large breasts and protruding nipples embarrassed me. In a rare move, she took the initiative, called and made reservations for the two of us for the workshop. It was given by some of the leading women thinkers of the time in conjunction with the book, *Our Bodies, Ourselves.*

We arrived a few minutes early at the Sheraton hotel in Cambridge. It felt strange to be alone with my mother. I usually did things alone with Dad. I didn't really know what to talk about and found the silence between us unnerving. Luckily it was not long before others showed up.

"Good Morning," said a tall thin blonde woman with a deep, rich voice that did not seem to match her matchstick thin body. "Here are your nametags. Find a seat wherever you are comfortable, and we'll get started very soon."

Mom and I took our nametags and sat on the left side of the room in the circle of chairs. She proudly placed her nametag over her right breast. I didn't put mine on as I have always had an aversion to nametags. The room was cold so I left my jacket on. Others began to come in, women around my mom's age and a bit younger. There weren't any other girls my age. I prayed someone my age would show up.

Carol, a thin brunette, stood in the middle of the circle and introduced herself and her co-leaders. "I'm thrilled to be here with you all today, to have a place where women can come together and talk openly and freely. It's been a long time coming. Let's get started." She spoke with the ebullience of a cheerleader.

We went around the room and said our names and who we were with. I was the only daughter with her mother. There were oohs and aahs from women who were delighted by my being there with my mother.

The room darkened, and Carol put up a projector of a nude woman's body. She discussed the joy of women's breasts and their breast tissues. She went on to talk about the need for good bras, no bras and self-exams. She put up a map of self-exams. Within minutes, she had us all examining our breasts. The room remained dark. I was thankful for that. Some women took off their bras and shirts, while others did the exam through their shirts. My mom looked straight ahead and did the breast exam through her shirt. I sat still. I was not about to touch anything. She never looked at me for my reaction. I was grateful.

Shortly after, Linda, a co-leader, discussed birth control for women and men. This discussion led to a talk on sexual pleasure. I got the idea that if one had good birth control, there would be more sexual pleasure. Up went pictures of sexual positions for achieving this pleasure that was a "woman's right". My face burned red hot. I prayed they'd never put the lights back on. I couldn't have dealt with anyone seeing my face, nor did I want to see my mother's face.

"We women," Carol said, "have earned the right to have sexual pleasure." As soon as the lights came back on, and we were given a bathroom break, I fled the room, avoiding meeting anyone's eye.

On my way back from the bathroom, Carol caught me off-guard. "It is so wonderful to have you with us today. It must be wonderful to have a mother like yours."

"Thank you," I said politely, staring at the cubist geometric shapes on the hotel's carpet.

As I walked back, Mom was talking with a few other women who beamed at me. I took my seat, took a deep breath and braced myself for the next part of the day. Mom and I never said a word to each other.

After lunch, there was a discussion about good gynecological health and the need for women to take charge of their health. As Carol was talking about our vaginas, Linda went around the room passing out mirrors, plastic gadgets, speculums, wipes and plastic bags.

When she got to my mother and me, she only had one speculum left. She said, "If you would share a toothbrush, then you can share this, as well."

I looked at the clear plastic speculum. Was she serious? My stomach tightened.

"Mom, I'm going to the bathroom." I went to the bathroom and then sat in the hallway until I saw other women coming out of the room.

My mom and I drove home in silence. I didn't want to ever speak about that workshop. I prayed my mother had the good sense not to tell my father what we did in the workshop.

I stayed up in my bedroom for most of the next day. I sat on my perch, smoked one Lark after another, and spoke with the old oak whose branches tickled my foot. "I don't know," I said, "Am I just being weird or was that a strange thing to bring a kid to? It was totally gross."

"It was definitely weird. Sometimes parents do weird things."

"Good, I was hoping it wasn't me." I took a deep drag.

I thought about the picture of my parents leaving for their honeymoon with my mother perfectly dressed, beaming with her rich red ruby lips and blunt bangs. That was the mother I wanted her to be. Every time my belly ached thinking of the workshop, I planted that picture in the front of my mind. I tried hard not to think of the mother who in the name of feminism walked around the house with her nipples protruding through her T-shirt. Or the mother whose hair looked like a rooster's mane when I came home from school because she had slept half the day away. Or the mother who never dared to speak up to her raging husband. I closed my eyes and felt the sun upon my face, and I savored the picture of my mom smiling.

Father

I was my father's favorite. He took me everywhere. When I was 9, just as spring was awakening, I was sitting in the den alone watching TV early one morning. Dad came in and said, "Come on, Ellie. We'll let everyone else sleep." We crept out of the house before the sun had risen and drove into Boston. We'd normally go to Haymarket Square as a family outing. The sunrise splayed pink and red strokes across the sky. It looked like giant ribbon candy weaving in and out of the tall city buildings.

When we arrived at Haymarket, the parking lot was almost empty. "Best spot of the day," Dad said as we pulled into our space. The smell of freshly cut grapefruit and sizzling kielbasa wafted through the air. My mouth watered and my stomach gurgled as we walked through the dirt parking lot to the outside edge of the old pushcarts. The first row was piled high with grapefruits, cantaloupes, bananas, oranges and pineapples. Behind the stalls were rows of boxes filled with fruit and vegetables. On warmer days, I'd stay away from this area because the produce would swelter in the sun and turn into a mushy, sour swamp that smelled like baby's puke. The next inner row of pushcarts was filled with cucumbers, tomatoes, red and green peppers, mushrooms, varieties of lettuce, bok choy and red and white cabbage. The men who owned the pushcarts were as colorful as their produce and loved to yell out their prices and slogans.

"Hey fat man," yelled the guy selling cucumbers. "Get ova here. I gotta special for ya today." My father and the cucumber man with the big bumpy nose always bantered. "I'll give you two for a buck."

"A buck?" he roared, "That's your big special?"

"Hey, I'll throw in an extra for your cute little girl."

"What about four for a quarter?"

"Do you want me to starve my children?"

"Alright, I'll give you fifty cents for these four."

"I might as well throw them to the birds. Help me out, here. A man's gotta live."

The cucumber man tossed four cucumbers in a paper bag and hurled the bag at my father saying, "Fahgettaboudit. Go live in peace."

My dad laughed, pulled two dollar bills from his customary thick wad of cash and gave it to him. He grabbed an empty box sitting next to the cart and said, "Next week, bring me a sweet deal."

A few carts away was Tony, the guy who sold cantaloupes. He had huge shoulders, a big head and a jowly face. He loved to chew on fat cigars. Half-standing and half-sitting on a high metal stool, he looked like a St. Bernard.

"Hey monster, whaddaya have today?" my father yelled as he sashayed through the crowd. I never knew why he called him monster but thought it was funny.

Tony turned, pulled his eyelids up and stretched his mouth super wide for my pleasure. "Aar." I giggled. "Get ova here and taste the sweetest cantaloupe of the year, betta than candy." He handed me a toothpick with a piece of cantaloupe.

I popped it in my mouth. "Mmm, better than candy."

"Alright, alright," my father interrupted, "whada you say Ellie, yes or no?"

"Yes, yes."

"Alright my man, cantaloupes it is for the little lady today." My father threw the bag of cantaloupes in the box with the cucumbers.

While I enjoyed the banter, my eye was on the real prize — the kielbasa that came at the end of these shopping sprees. I licked my lips just thinking about it.

Frankie, the owner of the meat shop, cooked on a simple oversized hot plate. The line for kielbasa wrapped around the old brick building for at least a block, sometimes two or even three. People never seemed to mind. While they waited they exchanged tales about Frankie.

Frankie, it seemed, had gotten into a drunken fight with his blonde-haired girlfriend over another guy looking at her. The night after the fight he went and robbed a bank. Some people say he did it to get even with her. Others argued he did it to impress her. Whatever the reason, he spent many years in prison for a bank robbery he did in his early 20s. When he got out, he supposedly bought the shop with the money he hid from the robbery. I always doubted this story. I couldn't imagine this sweet soft-spoken man robbing a bank.

"Hi Frankie, I'll have my usual please," I said. Frankie loomed over his hotplate like a tall stalk of corn. The men called him Stretch. I always called him Frankie.

He smiled, exposing pointed and crooked teeth that looked like baby shark's teeth. "Here's for my lady," he said handing me a kielbasa sample. "Tell me what ya think about this one."

I took a bite. "Mmm," I said, "Sweet and juicy. Just perfect. Thanks, Frankie."

"And thank you, my lady," he said and bowed to me as if I were a princess.

Frankie was not the only guy who had stories told about him at Haymarket Square. The market was rich in tales about bad guys. I was careful about believing any of them. Growing up in my family, I had learned how hurtful stories could be.

My father carried on talking and laughing with the vendors near Frankie's store. As I finished my kielbasa, I watched the penny players, Billy, Charlie, Tommy, Flat Top, and Arnie. Every Saturday, they sat on the sidewalk outside of Frankie's on metal folding chairs and cardboard boxes. They'd toss a penny towards the coke bottle on the cobblestone sidewalk covered with sawdust. Tommy always flipped the penny high between his thumb and his index finger. I used to think he created the game because he had so much finesse flipping it, but he lost a lot, so I was never sure. It didn't really matter. They'd razz each other as if they were still boys in high school. Billy, the most vocal of the group and the one with the biggest belly, would start the razzing session. "Oh, for God's sake Flat Top, still can't throw a penny? Can someone please teach the old boy to throw? Tommy, take him out back and teach him a thing or two, wouldja?"

"Well, at least I'm not still walking around with a belly big enough to float us all down the Rio Grande," chortled Flat Top.

"Now, girls, don't make me send ya home to your mommies," Tommy chided, sucking on a soggy cigar hanging out of the side of his mouth.

"Come on, Ellie. Let's get this stuff in the car," my father said.

"Can't we just watch them finish?"

"It'll be closing time before they'll finish. Come on. Let's go get everyone else and visit Bubbie and Nannie."

Dad threw the huge box filled with fruits and vegetables in the back of the wagon.

"I got three melons for my Ellen," he said as he tickled me.

"I've got a rad fruit just for my Dad."

"I got peach jelly, as sweet as my Ellie."

"We've got big full bellies." We laughed in unison as we drove away. It was such a treat to play with the "good" dad even though I knew the "bad" dad was always lurking just below the surface.

"Ah, my gunif is here," said my great grandmother, Bubbie, in a thick German accent. "You look good, my gunif." Bubbie was my father's paternal grandmother. She squeezed my father's cheek as he walked through the front door of her apartment. One by one my family filed in behind him like a flock of ducks for our Sunday visit.

Bubbie Close was the only person we addressed by both her first and last name. I never knew why, but I liked how it sounded and felt. She was so bow-legged she walked with two canes, which she used to give you a swift nudge if she thought you needed it. She had on her customary house dress overlaid with a powdery blue cashmere sweater with tiny white beads. All of her dresses looked the same, two deep pockets in the front and a zipper up the back with snaps at the top. The top snap was always undone. The pockets were overfilled with Bubbie's stuff: a tiny comb for her thin white hair that was pulled up in a small bun, an overstuffed billfold held together by a thick elastic band, a handful of change, a small scoring pencil, a magnifying glass and one piece of hard butterscotch candy.

I was the last one to file in through the door. She looked around, pulled a silver whiskey flask out from her bosom and took a good swig. She then pulled her sparkly satchel of money from her brassiere and slipped me a five dollar bill. With a gummy grin, she whispered in Yiddish, "Ay Shayna madel, Vas ves good, yah yiddersher kop ya." *Ay, my pretty girl with a smart head.* I knew she meant, *You're so smart, you won't tell anyone our secret, right?* I smiled and shook my head.

I ran into the kitchen looking for Bubbie's candy stash and ginger ale. My mother was standing there.

"What's gunif mean?" I asked.

"Never mind."

"Come on, Mom. Tell me. What does it mean?"

"Ellen, forget it."

"Mom, please." I pulled a can of ginger ale out of the refrigerator.

"It means gangster. There, are you happy now? It's Yiddish for gangster."

Even though Bubbie's house was always 100 degrees and had a musty, old-people smell, I felt at home. We could plop all over the furniture, rummage through her refrigerator and find treats. She always had a stash of candy waiting for us in a surprise corner of her apartment. Her small blue eyes would open with a childlike wonder. "Aay, vat do we have here?" she'd squeal. We were always so proud of ourselves for finding such good loot.

Our next stop after Bubbie Close's was Nannie's house. We all piled back in the station wagon to go to Nannie's a few towns away.

"Dad, do we have to go there today?" I asked.

"Ellen, be nice. She's your grandmother."

"But she's not nice."

"She's just tired and old."

"But Bubbie Close is way older, and she's nice."

"Ellen, we're going, and you're going to be polite. Do you hear me?"

"Yeah, I hear you."

At Nannie's, we were supposed to be quiet and stay out of her way. Nannie was a large woman with flabby arms that hung off of her. I thought she looked like her refrigerator: tall, square and cold with a rounding at her shoulders. Whenever we visited, she was always cooking with her back to us. We always had to visit her at her house. She never came to ours. She had a lot of rules. We had to sit on the furniture that was covered in a thick plastic. Everything was covered in plastic. It always made the back of my legs sweat, and I'd stick to it. When I complained to my mother once about Nanny being so cranky and mean, she said we needed to be nice to her because she had been sick with cancer for a long time.

"She has eyes on the back of her head," I whispered to my brother Robert as we crouched behind the sofa.

"What are you two doing?" Nannie called. She was stirring the boiling chicken soup in the adjoining kitchen, but she still knew we were up to something.

"Nothing," I said as we both popped more candy in our mouths. We'd found coffee nibs in the back of the drawer of the telephone desk in the front hall.

"You're not eating candy, are you?"

My eyes opened wide. I smiled at my brother. "You see."

"Nope," I said with my mouth full.

"You'd better not be eating candy," she said, never turning to look at us.

Robert and I covered our mouths with our hands. We laughed so hard we were snorting coffee juice out of our nostrils. After catching my breath, I realized Nannie was no longer standing in front of the stove in the kitchen.

"Where's Nannie?" I whispered. Robert shrugged. "Did she melt?"

My mother was occupied playing Cat's Cradle with my younger brothers and sister.

"Come on," I said. We spied on the kitchen. Nannie was not there. I pointed down the hall to Robert and tiptoed towards her bedroom. Angry voices came from behind the nearly closed door. I curled my index finger, motioning to Robert for us to get closer. He shook his head no. I went ahead by myself.

"Ay Lenny," I heard Nannie say. "Will nothing ever change with you?"

"Ma, I…"

"Once a bum, always a bum." From the slit in the door, I could see my grandmother's arms folded and my father's shoes pointing in towards each other.

"Ma, you're not…"

"Lenny, enough. I have heard enough." Yet again Nannie was making him feel bad. She was always cutting him down, saying hateful things.

I scooted down the hall back to the living room. "Mom, I don't feel good. Can you get Dad?"

"Ellen, Dad's talking to Nannie. He won't be long."

"My stomach hurts."

"Well, if you didn't eat all that candy, it wouldn't hurt. Go sit down on the sofa and rest. It'll feel better."

I sat on the couch and folded my arms. Nothing would ever feel better at Nannie's house.

My grandmother loved to tell stories about my father. Her stories made my stomach queasy. Even though they were often funny, they ended up with my father doing something bad. She was always insulting him in front of us. She never had a good word to say about him. I often wondered why my grandmother detested my father. Even when he was young, she was mean to him. How my father was treated by his parents was part of our family lore. We all knew the stories. As a boy, he was made to sleep out on the porch in Boston's frigid winter months. For years, he had to wear cardboard in his shoes because his parents refused to give him proper footwear, even though his father, Bob, owned a clothing store that sold shoes. We all knew how his mother threw him out of the house when he was 13, while his sister Louisa was being primped and primed for a debutante party. Nannie would say that girls needed to be taken care of while boys could take care of themselves. Bob must have felt the same way. He didn't pay any attention to my father at all. Somehow, they expected my father to bring himself up.

When I was 12, I heard an unfamiliar sniffling coming from my parents' bedroom. The door was almost closed. I slowly opened it. My father stood staring at the tie rack on the closet door. Tears ran down both sides of his cheeks. I had never seen my father cry.

"Dad, what's wrong?"

"Nannie died, Ellie. She's gone," he said with his head down.

I reached up on my tiptoes to give him a hug. "It'll be okay," I said, even though I knew it wouldn't be. My father morphed into a soft little boy in a big man's body before my eyes. It scared me. He was small and vacant. I wanted my big, boisterous "good" father back.

"Ellie, what tie do you think I should wear? Pick me a tie, would you?"

There were dozens of overlapping ties in every possible color, solid, striped, polka dotted. I couldn't seem to choose. Finally, I picked a blue and red striped one and handed it to him. He fumbled as he tied it.

"Where are you going?"

"I need to go and make funeral arrangements."

"Can I come?"

"No, Ellie, you stay here with your mother."

My stomach twisted into a ball as my father left for the funeral home. I could feel how sad he was, and there was nothing I could do to make it better. After he left, I walked down to the kitchen. My mother sat at the table, smoking and drinking coffee. She turned to me and said, "Nannie told your father she never loved him while she was in the hospital. Even on her death bed, she couldn't bring herself to be kind to him. I really don't know why she just couldn't love him." My mother took a hard drag of her Salem and shook her head.

My father had a best friend we called Uncle Sal. He was a short, stocky, Sicilian man with a wide lopsided nose. My dad often took my brothers and me to Sal's place in the basement of an old narrow building in Little Italy. There were three steep cement steps going down into Sal's place. My father breathed heavily and held onto the sidewall for balance as he maneuvered his weight, shifting side to side, down each step. When he got to the bottom, he banged on the metal grate. A heavy-set man smoking a cigar named Willy would open the door. He didn't speak much and never said hello.

Sal's place consisted of two rooms. The front room had a small TV in the corner that was always on and a big round table where most of his friend's would sit, play cards and smoke thick cigars. In the back room, a dim light hung above an old wooden desk with a metal lamp and a beige phone. Behind the desk sat an old worn-out leather chair, and smaller wooden chairs sat in front of it. A small dirty window with a heavy black metal grate let in the only daylight in the basement. A yellowed calendar hung by a nail on the cracked gray wall.

"Ellie, I'm going to go talk with Sal. You stay here," my father said as he walked into the backroom and partially closed the door. The older men at the round table played a game my brother told me was called Black Jack. I didn't understand the game but enjoyed tracking the men's banter.

"Oh, for God's sake," the guy smoking the thickest cigar said. "What do you think? You're playing with your mother? For God's sake we don't have all day."

"Alright boys," said Gus, a tall, bony guy with sunken cheeks who was always at Sal's.

"Fahgettaboudit," a short stalky guy said, throwing down his cards. He looked like Sal. "I'm out. Ya happy now?"

"What ya need is a pair of diapers," said the fat guy sitting closest to the back room.

I burst out laughing. They turned and looked at me. I felt like my face had a bad sunburn and stopped giggling.

"Just rememba boys, we got a visita here. Capiche?" said Gus.

I'd sneak peeks of my father and Sal talking in the backroom. My father's arms were flying around. I asked Dad once what they talked about in private. He said it was business. I watched as he handed a fat white envelope full of cash to Uncle Sal. Secretly, I was proud he had so much money to give to Uncle Sal.

When they were done talking, Sal came out and came up to me, grabbing me for one of his bear hugs. "Come here," he said in a thick, husky Bostonian-Italian accent. "How's my little girl?"

"Good," I smiled. I liked Sal very much.

"You're gonna have to be careful with this one," he said to my dad. "She's getting too pretty." I blushed and giggled.

"Good," said Sal. "You're a good kid. Stay good."

We left Sal's and drove home along Route 9. "I gotta go out of town next week for business," Dad said.

"Where are you going?" I asked.

"Overseas."

"Where?"

"England."

I became quiet. Business or no business, I didn't like him going away. I didn't feel safe in the house without him. Sometimes, of course, I didn't feel safe with him there, but between my mother and my father, I felt much safer with him at home. My mother was too unstable to protect us if anything happened. This was just one of the many contradictions living under the roof of an abusive father and a mentally ill mother. Even though I begged her to leave him, I didn't feel safe alone with her. It was a dark conundrum.

My mother also hated when he left every couple of months. She didn't sleep well. She'd drink more and eat less, stay up all night and remain in bed later each morning. I'd have to do more of the cooking and cleaning and make sure the kids had packed lunches. I couldn't get the smell of booze and stale cigarettes out of the downstairs of the house, and I couldn't erase the demons the booze brought upon my mother.

"I'll be back before you know it." My father squeezed me closer to him as we drove. "You'll see."

"What are you going to do there?"

"I'm going to visit the Queen of England."

"No, seriously, Dad, what are you going to do?"

"Seriously, that's what I'm going to do." We pulled up in front of our house. "Ellie, why don't you go see if your mother needs help with dinner."

One of the greatest challenges growing up with my father was that you never knew what to expect. One moment, he was the funny fat man laughing and playing with you, while the next he was this crazy man, exploding like a hand grenade. There was no rhyme or reason to his craziness. I wonder if he ever made sense out of his madness. When he got set off, there was no way of knowing when or what would make it stop. His moods truly seemed out of his control.

At dinner that night, he picked up his dish and threw it in my mother's direction and screamed, "What is this shit? You call this food? What the fuck's the matter with you?"

Dinnertime seemed to be one of the consistent triggers. All of us could be sitting at the table laughing and joking when all of a sudden his rage exploded.

The plate flew past my mother and hit the wall. She didn't

move. "Do you hear me, Jack? I'm talking to you." His face turned a dark, purple red and his eyes bulged. "What's the matter? Cat got your tongue?"

"I…" my mother tried to say something.

"I, I, I didn't mean to give you this fucking food for dinner. Is that what you're going to tell me? Just get the fuck out of here and leave us all alone."

She pushed her chair away from the table and left. None of us moved. I wanted to run after her but knew not to. One of us was next on his chopping block.

"Eat," my father said.

My siblings began to eat on his command. I lost my appetite, couldn't even force myself to eat. Pushing the food around my plate and praying he wouldn't notice, I tried to make an escape plan in my head. Could I run out the back door? No, it was too close to where he was sitting. I wished I could jump in the dryer and spin around until it was really hot and dinner was over, but I remembered that was how our cats died.

"Ellen, stop playing with that food," he screamed.

I stood up.

"Sit down and eat," he ordered.

"How do you expect me or anyone else to eat?" I yelled. Of all the kids, I was the one who usually gave it to him. Still, it was the first time I was ever this direct. I knew I was his favorite, but that didn't ever stop him from using his belt on me. I actually seemed to get it worse than most of the other kids.

The floor below me no longer felt sturdy. I became lightheaded. My knees went weak. I tried to focus on the items in the kitchen wallpaper to help me to stay strong. How many things are in that wallpaper? An iron, a kettle, a…

"So help me God, sit down, and eat your dinner."

"I can't," I cried. "Look at what you've done." I pointed at the spaghetti dripping off the wall onto the rug. I ran upstairs to my bedroom on the third floor.

"Get down here right now," he screamed after me. "We are not done. Ellen, so help me God. You get down here right now."

There was a dead silence after his last scream. I knew I was in for it, but I no longer cared. I felt cold and numb. I just couldn't sit there and eat. Getting a beating seemed easier.

As I curled up into a ball on my bed with the blankets piled on top of me, I worried about my brothers and sister still sitting there with him. I listened intently but heard nothing. The silence spooked me more than his screaming. When I couldn't stand it any longer, I crept down the red-carpeted stairs and listened. It was so quiet. Someone's fork dropped against a plate. I jumped. "Fuck," I thought to myself, "What am I supposed to do now?"

His silence was more punishing than his blood curdling screams. I ran back upstairs to try and figure out what to do. As soon as I got up to my room, he screamed, "Ellen, get down here right now."

I was relieved. When I got downstairs, he was still sitting at the head of the table. He picked up his fork and pointed to the wall. "Clean this shit up."

I didn't say a word and cleared the table, relieved to see my brothers and sister in one piece. Everyone ran upstairs to their bedrooms. My father grabbed a box of Oreo cookies, a glass of milk and his secret stash of candy from the kitchen cabinet. He tucked it under his left armpit and left the kitchen. Parked himself on the couch and inhaled the entire bag of candy big enough for our entire family. It was his nightly ritual. He'd never share. Even the slightest hint that one of us might want a piece of his stash could bring on a verbal lashing that would obliterate any sense of being.

I was happy to be left alone. As I washed the spaghetti off the wall and the carpet, I wondered when I would get my beating with his worn out black leather belt. Out of the corner of my eye, I watched him suffocating himself, intoxicating himself and prayed I'd never turn out like him.

By the time I was done, he was fully occupied with his stash and some movie he was watching. I knew he'd soon be done with his bag, his eyes would get heavy and his breathing would become deep and slow. He'd fall asleep, and my world would be safe and calm. I walked upstairs. The entire house was quiet and at ease.

In my father's fashion, nothing was ever said about this evening. By the next morning he was the happy fun Dad again, and we were all expected to forget about the episode and be cheerful.

"Good morning, Ellie," he said, patting my head as I walked down the stairs. His touch sent a chill through my body. "Something wrong?"

"Nope. Morning," I said and ran down the stairs, grabbed my knapsack and sprinted out the front door to school.

He left for England the next day. In the middle of the next week, we got a call from him. He told my mother to put me on the phone.

"How are you, Ellie?"

"Okay. I miss you. When are you coming home?"

"Very soon. I have someone very special who wants to speak with you."

"Who?"

"The Queen of England."

"No way, Dad."

"Here," he said, "Wait one moment."

"Hello," said a woman with an English accent. "Is this Ellen?"

"Yes."

"This is the Queen of England."

"Oh, it's very nice to speak with you."

"And to you as well," she said and handed the phone back to my father.

"Dad, who was that really?"

"The Queen of England. I need to go now, Ellie. I'll be home soon. I love you. Bye."

I never really knew if the woman I spoke to was indeed the Queen of England. I couldn't imagine what my father would have to do with the Queen. But there was so much about his business I didn't understand. Anything was possible.

My father took many business trips overseas for the next few months. At most, he'd be gone two weeks. He spent time in the Middle East. He always came home with enchanting stories of Shahs and kings. And great presents.

One of my favorite stories was how he drank this black muddy coffee with Shahs in a place called Qatar. He presented me with my own Turkish cup rimmed in white gold.

"You drank from the same cup? Gross," I said, rolling my finger around the rim of the cup.

"Oh Ellie, according to their customs, it would have been very rude not to, perhaps even dangerous."

"Oh," was all I could manage.

The men wore long white dresses and wrapped their heads in a red and white material with a black cloth on top. My head swirled as I tried to imagine the scenes and places he spoke of. As hard as I tried, the men seemed more like genies in fairy tales than real people.

I held the cup up to my nose, closed my eyes and summoned up the smell of thick black coffee, dark Arabian men and dusty dirt roads taken on camelback.

For years, I wondered what a fat American Jewish man was doing sharing coffee with Shahs and kings in the Middle East. After my father's death, my mother told me he was selling arms. She learned about his dealings by listening in on his phone calls. When I asked her if she ever confronted him, she said, "Are you crazy? You know your father. You could never confront him about anything."

He continued to travel to faraway, mysterious places for business. From Switzerland, he brought me one of my most treasured gifts, a red woolen skating dress lined in crimson silk. It had two hand embroidered lines of white flowers running down each side. I walked around hugging the dress the entire day, brought it to the dinner table and took it to sleep with me that night. Skating meant everything to me. I dreamed about becoming an Olympic skating star.

One Sunday, my father took me to skate at the outdoor rink in downtown Boston at the Prudential Center. I flew onto the ice in my fancy new red dress as if I were Dorothy Hamill. As I did my circle of back crossovers with one-legged arabesques and made attempts at camel spins, my heart soared. My father stood on the sidelines yelling "10.0! 10.0!" I smiled and squealed with delight. After a few more circles around the rink, I noticed he was talking to a man in a long gray coat and black figure skates. I had seen him skating in the rink earlier. When I took a hot chocolate break, my father told me that the man was involved with the Skating Club of Boston. He told my father that he should bring me to the Club as he felt I showed real promise. I was beside myself. I was one step closer to achieving my dream of becoming an Olympic skating star. I got to skate for the entire two hour session without Dad making me quit early as he had a bad habit of doing. On the drive home, I imagined going to the Skating Club and being recognized as an Olympic hopeful.

"Dad," I blurted, "when can you take me to meet that man from the Skating Club?" He was silent. "Dad, when can we go?"

"Did you put the heat up?" he asked.

"No."

"Did I tell you you could put the heat up?" he screamed.

"Dad, I...."

"What the fuck's the matter with you, Ellen?"

I pulled on my jacket zipper and bit my lip. "Dad..."

"What's wrong with you, Ellen? What the fuck's the matter with you, honestly?"

"Nothing, I didn't..."

"Don't fucking talk to me, Ellen."

I moved as close to the door as I could get without jumping out of the car. I shrunk down inside myself and tried to make sense out of what was going on. We drove home in suffocating silence.

He never took me to the Skating Club. It was never spoken of again.

Just as winter was bowing to spring, I awoke one morning well before dawn to a dark house that had a strange empty feeling. It was too quiet. I walked downstairs and noticed no one was in my parent's bedroom. I took a deep breath and continued down to the kitchen. The smell of stale cigarettes and booze permeated the air.

My mother sat in the dark, slumped over the table, clutching a half filled drinking glass in her left hand and a cigarette in her right. On the table was an oversized bottle of vodka and our blue plastic water pitcher filled with orange juice. My father's green glass oyster ashtray was overfilled with cigarette butts. It reminded me of the old cemetery with too many headstones keeled over, crashing into one another. My mother had her powdery blue nightgown on with a pair of untied brown leather shoes. I thought, she should at least have socks on. Her thick black hair stood up on the top of her head like a rooster's mane.

"Mom," I ask nervously, "Where's Dad?"

"He left us, Ellen. That son of a bitch left us. Now what are we going to do, Ellen?"

A huge alarm bell went off inside of me, "What do you mean he left?"

"That's what I mean. He's gone." She lit another Salem.

I put a kettle on the stove to make her a cup of coffee. I prayed I'd get her sober before the other kids woke up.

"We have nothing," she slurred, "Do you hear me, nothing."

"Mom, it'll be okay," I lied.

"Don't be so naive. It won't be okay. He left us with no money. I have no money to feed you kids with. How could he do this to me? I have nobody to go to. Nobody, do you hear me?"

I put a brown mug filled with black coffee on the table in front of her.

"I don't need coffee." She pushed it away.

"Mom, did he tell you where he was going?"

"To England," she said bluntly. My stomach fell out from under me the same way it did when I rode the rollercoaster at Nantasket Beach. "Mom, you need to drink this coffee, please."

"I'm so sorry you have to have a mother like me, Ellen. You deserve better," she said, breaking into large sobs.

"Mom, just drink the coffee, please."

"Look at me, you deserve better than this."

"Yes," I wanted to scream. "Yes, I fucking deserve a lot better than all of this." But I remained silent, praying to not set her off any worse than she already was.

"Mom, what happened?"

"You know your father, Ellen. Since when did he need a reason for anything? He just does whatever he wants to do. Period. End of story."

"But Mom, he wouldn't just leave. He's never just left."

"Well, he did. Didn't he?"

I couldn't believe he'd leave us without saying goodbye. I knew he loved me enough to at least say goodbye. None of it made any sense. Waves of nausea rolled through my body. I leaned against the table to steady myself.

For the next few weeks, I pondered my father's leave-taking in my journal. I wrote him countless furious letters that he'd never receive. I wrote as many letters to God begging for his help. Some of my prayers were answered. One of them came in the form of help from Uncle Phil, my father's rich uncle. He came with enough money every few weeks so we could eat, pay the rent and keep the lights on. But my other prayers didn't seem to be getting answered. Weeks went by without even a whisper from my father.

I rummaged through my father's papers to figure out where in England he had gone. I started in the most obvious place, his dark mahogany desk in the living room. I didn't really know what I was looking for. Many of the papers had numbers added up in long columns. Some had numbers jotted everywhere. He would have killed me for looking through his stuff.

With each passing week, my mother drank more. Her moods worsened. I found her one night smoking a cigar. She had run out of cigarettes. I had to take over the role of mother for my younger siblings. My stomach ached on a daily basis. When I found no clues in my father's desk, I ransacked the front closets. In one, I found a metal box that was locked and a gun shoved behind a black T-shirt. It scared me to death. Guns had always scared me. I never knew my father had a gun. Did my mother know about it? The conversation between Bubbie Close and my father rang in my head. Was he really a gunif? Scared that I had touched it, I shoved the gun back with a blue and brown cashmere scarf. I prayed I'd forget it was there and that my father hadn't done anything wrong. Afraid of what else I might find, I stopped rummaging through the house for the next few days. But this did not last long.

Hours were spent in my bedroom thinking of where I might find information on his whereabouts. The remaining obvious places were the attic, the basement, his dresser and his closet. I could go through the attic anytime during the day without disturbing the ghost who I was convinced lived there. The basement would take courage, though, as I was afraid of the dark empty rooms. His dresser and closet needed to be done without my mother's knowledge.

The next evening, while my mother was getting dinner together that would end up tasting like Palmolive dish detergent as so many of her meals did in those days, I went into my parent's bedroom and started in the closet. My father was a clothes horse, and his clothes crowded out my mother's. I looked in the back on the floor, rummaging through their shoes. There were no papers, but I did find a one hundred dollar bill. I shoved it into my back pocket just in case Uncle Phil stopped coming.

In his pants and coat pockets, I found three crumpled white handkerchiefs glued together with stale snot. My father suffered from hay fever and was constantly heaving huge snot-filled sneezes. I had inherited his monster sneezes, but thankfully not his hay fever. People, including me, often laughed and jumped when I sneezed.

In one of his coat pockets was an empty envelope with numbers jotted on it. I tried dialing the numbers and got busy signals. I found tons of loose change that I decided to save. In one of his last pant pockets, I came across a tan ponytail holder. It wasn't mine. I would never have owned a tan colored holder. It would either be black to match my hair or two colors twisted together as an accent to my hair. It wasn't my mother's. Her hair was too short. Why did my father have such a holder in his pocket? I didn't like this holder, didn't even want to touch it. In my parents' bathroom, I got some toilet paper, wrapped the holder in it and shoved it in my back pocket to figure it out later.

I smelled the meatloaf cooking and knew that I needed to move onto the dresser if I wanted to get through it that day. On top was an ornate sterling silver frame with the picture of my parents driving off for their honeymoon that I loved so much. They looked like movie stars. My mother was like a starlet of the fifties. My father with his six foot three stature was leading-man material. Together they were dazzling.

Sitting next to the frame was an unopened miniature bottle of Vodka that he got on some plane ride, some pennies, an oversized paperclip and a small bottle of English Leather cologne. The top part of my father's dresser opened outward to expose narrow drawers. It was an expensive, finely made piece of furniture they got when they were just married, but age and slamming had worn the tracks. The drawers opened with a stutter.

I found graying underwear with overstretched bands and holes, yellowed T-shirts, black socks with gold toes, and white handkerchiefs. In the bottom drawer, there was a black leather binder of unused baby blue checks with canceled checks stuffed in the back. I pulled it out and put it on my parent's bed to examine it. Going through the stacks, I found many checks written to a Karen Schlesinger, many for large amounts, the largest for $10,000.

Staring at them, I just knew. I knew she was the reason he was in England. I hated him. I detested her. How could she take a man away from his children? This was our money he was sending her. I wanted to rip the checks into shreds, but knew they must be kept intact as proof. My mother needed to know what was going on.

Overtaken with a feeling of revenge against this woman, I wanted to make her hurt as badly as I was hurting. Images of her laughing with my father as my mother cried herself to sleep

pleaded with my mother for years to leave him, had begged him to come home.

Still, once he was home, I resented him asserting himself again as my father. No longer his little girl, I had grown up well beyond my chronological age while he was gone. Having survived without a father, I didn't need or want one now.

By the following spring, my family seemed to be back to life as it had always been. I even managed to let go of my resentments toward my father. There was less fighting between my parents. My father's moods were less erratic. Life was good. It was a peaceful time.

One day, as I walked home from school, I passed my favorite jasmine tree in full bloom. I stopped and put my nose into a jasmine flower. There was nothing better than the sweet scent. Turning the corner onto our street, I saw five black sedans in front of our house. My stomach fell. My knees went weak. Something was wrong. I ran as fast as my feet would take me. Inside the house, it was too quiet. I ran to the kitchen.

My father was seated at the table. I scanned the room. Three men sat across from him and two men were on either side of him. They wore blue suits, white shirts and ties. A badge was attached to the side of one of the men's belt. My father was too quiet, looked weary and had fear in his eyes. His hands were folded in front of him on the table.

"Dad, what's going on?"

"Ellie, these men are from the FBI and are here to talk with me."

My mind couldn't manage to keep up. FBI? FBI? My heart pounded against my chest. I wanted to reach out and touch him but was too afraid to. If I touched him the scene would somehow become real.

Everything was in its right place, yet it all felt so wrong. The oversized white washing machine and dryer still sat behind the kitchen table. The brown wooden kitchen cabinets looked just like our cabinets. The orange-brown wall-to-wall rug was there with all its familiar stains. I could smell cigarette smoke coming from the bathroom adjacent to the kitchen.

"Ha," my mother screamed from behind the bathroom door in her crazy voice. "Tell her the truth, Lennie."

Hearing my mother's voice, I wanted to vomit. I tried to keep it together.

"Ellie, they have some questions about some business that I have been involved with."

"Ha, they're interrogating him, Ellen," my mother screamed.

The FBI men didn't change their expressions. They didn't seem to notice or care about my mother screaming. They sat tall, still and serious. There was something scary about these men in blue suits with crisp, clean haircuts. I ran into the bathroom. My mother was ripping up papers and flushing them down the toilet. Several cigarettes were burned down in the sink.

"Mom, what are you doing?" I grabbed her arm.

"They're going to take him away, Ellen. They're going to take him away."

"Mom, stop. Stop." I grabbed her with both arms.

"They want to take him away, Ellen. Over my dead body. You're not taking him," she screamed at the FBI men.

"Mom, shhh. This isn't going to help. Shhh." She burst into tears and fell into my arms. "It'll be okay. Come on, Mom, shhh." I put the toilet seat cover down. She sat, grabbed a Salem out of the pack and lit it. I went back into the kitchen and listened to the men barraging my father with questions.

"Where were you on the night of September 15th?"

"Did you have any dealings with Frankie the Enforcer or Buddy Harrell?"

They showed my father picture after picture of various people and places. "Do you know him? Or him? Have you been here? What do you know about this man?"

Barely able to breathe, I kept looking at him sitting so still at the table with his hands folded. He looked pale and shrunken as if he were an oversized kid trying to be good at detention hall. I prayed the FBI men could not see his fear, and I wondered why they never asked me to leave the room. I was a 15-year-old kid, and I knew I shouldn't be there.

"Do you know this man?" asked the agent sitting directly across from my father. He passed him a large photo of Uncle Sal. What did Uncle Sal have to do with all of this? I didn't know then that Uncle Sal was a hit man for the Mafia. I found that out when I was 17.

The interrogation lasted a few hours. When they were done, they collected all their pictures and materials and packed them back into their matching brief cases. One of the FBI men concluded by saying to my father, "Thank you for your cooperation." My father remained seated. They got up from the kitchen table in an eerie silence and let themselves out. I was relieved when the front door closed.

My father looked at me and said, "What about pizza for dinner, Ellie?"

My mother came out of the bathroom. She looked at my father and burst into tears. He gave her a gentle hug and said, "It's over Jackie. I'm here. I'm not going anywhere. Let's go get some pizza."

Nothing more was ever said.

Outsider

My 4th grade teacher, Sister Mary Ellen McDonald, stood erect like a fine platoon sergeant at the front of our white-washed classroom. Behind her desk loomed a six-foot cross as thick as a railroad tie, it smelled musty like old creosote-treated timber ties. It was her personal cross. She'd brought it in at the beginning of the year. She also brought a crazy-looking cherub with puffy cheeks and a red glass apple with a green stem, both of which sat on the edge of her desk. I imagined the cherub coming alive and having a head-spinning demonic outburst like Linda Blair in the Exorcist.

Holding a long wooden chalkboard pointer, Sister Mary Mack — as we called her behind her back — tapped her desk twice. My classmates and I rose in unison, faced the American flag, and with our right hands over our hearts, gave allegiance to the United States of America. We sat back into our seats with the swift staccato of a good platoon squad. My nostrils tingled and throat itched from inhaling the latent fumes of Clorox Bleach seeping from my desk. I coughed loudly, breaking the silence. Sister's obsession with cleanliness was second only to her fixation with Jesus Christ, her lord savior. Under the Boston public school system rules, she was allowed to wear her full habit. I was certain in her mind we were all novitiates, entering her monastery under her direct tutelage for our first year of postulancy.

"Please fold your hands for the Lord's Prayer," Sister instructed.

I put my hands on my lap. All the other students folded their hands on top of their desks. Sister began the daily prayer, "Our father who art in Heaven…" I remained silent.

"Miss Close, please stand."

I stood.

"Miss Close, would you care to join the rest of us in the Lord's Prayer today?" she asked, folding her pudgy arms through her white bell-shaped cotton sleeve.

"No, thank you, Sister. I pray to my God at Temple. Thank you, Sister."

Her face grew tight and red. She grabbed a ruler and slapped it against her fatty palm. "Miss Close, I have tolerated your poor behavior for as long as I care to. You may go to the principal's office immediately."

I held my head up proudly, turned and marched myself to the principal's office.

Mrs. Flynn was at her desk when I entered. She swiveled to face me. Her furrowed brow pushed up thick black pointy glasses. I wanted to laugh but didn't. "Yes, Miss Close?"

"Sister Mary Ellen McDonald sent me here for not saying her prayer to her God. I go to Temple every Friday night, and that's where I pray to God." I took a deep breath and glanced at the black telephone sitting on her desk. "You can call my parents if you don't believe me."

"Thank you, Miss Close. You may now go back to class. Please tell Sister you have been excused."

"Thank you." I turned and left her office smirking, practically running back to class. As I entered, Sister looked at me with her piercing blue eyes and said, "Oh, I see you've decided to join us once again."

"Yes," I said, walking towards my desk in the second row. "Mrs. Flynn told me to tell you that I have been excused from the Lord's Prayer."

She stood up and took her place next to her personal wooden cross. I imagined splinters entering my hand if I ever dared touch it. I never did. "Have a seat, Miss Close."

"Yes, Sister."

The next day, Sister's cross was gone. My parents never mentioned anything, but I knew they were behind it. I'd overheard my father saying that the nuns should not be permitted to wear their habits at school because it violated the U.S. Constitution. "If I had anything to do with it, they'd all have to take their habits off once and for all. It is a public school, for God's sake."

Sister Mary Mack continued to say the Lord's Prayer. Each day, I remained silent. Despite my initial victory, I remained petrified of her. She ruled our class like a fierce marine sergeant. If anyone got out of hand, she had no qualms about using the ruler on them. School codes existed that permitted her to hit younger children (under 6th grade) with the ruler on the fatty part of their palms, to hit older "troublemakers" on their knuckles, and to use the paddle on really bad kids. There were rumors she paddled a 6th grade boy in front of the class until he peed in his pants.

Each day, I brought with me my "Sister insurance" — extra sharpened pencils. The only sharpener in the room was attached to her desk. To use it, I would've had to turn my backside towards her.

Years later, I learned that ours was the very last class to be taught by nuns in full habit in Massachusetts public schools. Daily prayer was also abolished. I couldn't help but feel personally victorious.

A Jewish kid taught by nuns was rare, but to be the only Jewish family living in an all-Christian neighborhood in the suburbs of Boston was unheard of. Boston was made up of enclaves of people of the same color, ethnic background and union affiliation, as well as similar religious and political beliefs. People knew not to cross lines. West Roxbury was no different. It was often described as a suburb within a city.

West Roxbury was mostly Irish. If you weren't Irish Catholic, you were at least Christian. I don't know how many Jews lived in West Roxbury, but I was the only Jewish kid in my grade.

The Irish Catholic families sent their kids to the schools associated with the two large parishes at either end of the neighborhood. Most of the people owned their homes. We rented. The houses on our street were large but not lavish, accommodating large Irish Catholic families. Lots of firemen, policemen and teachers lived in our neighborhood.

Our house, a white colonial with black trim, was one of the more modest houses on the block. It had a large side yard, though, with two old Maples that offered shade on the hottest summer days and enough leaves in the fall to create huge mounds to jump into before we burned them. To this day, I can summon the bittersweet smell of burning leaves against the backdrop of the crisp autumn air.

Center Street was the main downtown thoroughfare. It had a small town feeling with a penny candy store, a hardware store, a bakery and a Woolworth's.

While I didn't want to belong to Sister's Catholic order at school, in my neighborhood there was one Christian tradition I craved — the celebration of Christmas. Each Christmas, our neighborhood turned into a magical winter wonderland. Six to eight inches of fresh snow blanketed the houses and streets, a perfect canvas against which the lights and trees could sparkle. The snow made the world move in slow motion. Sounds and lights were accentuated. Listening to boots crunching the fresh snow was hypnotic. At night, I lay in bed and watched snowflakes cartwheel through the crisp night sky and descend upon my windowpane in the shape of stars and diamonds. I could practically hear the stars twinkling.

In our neighborhood, it seemed like Christmas began the day after Thanksgiving and carried on until we returned to school in January when the trees were taken to the dump. I'd go over to play at Cathleen's house the weekend of Thanksgiving. At my request, we'd sit on their curvy eggplant velvet sofa and play Old Maid while we watched her parents pull boxes from the cellar marked XMAS. Cathleen's mom would hold up an ornament, looking at it as if she was viewing it for the first time and say: "Girls look at this. Isn't this just the most beautiful ballerina you've ever seen? She's going to look just perfect on the tree. Don't you think so?"

One part of me wanted to caress every ornament while another part fantasized about crushing them or worse, stealing them. My mind raced with images of the ballerina *accidently* falling into my coat pocket.

Ornaments weren't the only thing I wanted to steal. I wanted to steal Cathleen's mommy. Cathleen's mommy was happy, joyous and took special care with all the little details like tree trimming.

"Would you be a dear and put her on the end table?" she asked as she leaned towards me, holding the ballerina in her right hand.

I hesitated and pretended not to hear her. Oh God, what if I lost control and shoved her in my coat pocket or worse, grabbed her and ran out the door? I needed to do something so Cathleen's mom wouldn't think I was weird. I took a deep breath, smiled and gently took the ballerina and placed her on the end table next to the couch.

"Thank you dear. That's perfect."

I wanted to scream, "It's not perfect. There's nothing perfect about any of this. It's not perfect that I don't get to celebrate Christmas, that I don't get to have my own Christmas tree and that I don't have a happy mommy. There's nothing perfect about any of this."

Pretending to be somebody else, a somebody who belonged there, I imagined God watching me from above whispering, "Phony, real big phony." And yet I wanted it to be true for me. I wanted everything Christmas represented: a normal, happy family with a joy-filled life that sparkled just like the Christmas lights and tree ornaments.

Every evening as dusk fell over our neighborhood my heart sank as all the other houses magically came alive in green, blue, red and yellow lights. My neighbor's lights spewed diamond shaped colors across my bedroom wall. I could not escape Christmas.

But this was not the worst part. The most tortuous aspect was the inevitable Christmas tree. Wherever we went, we were reminded of the tree we weren't allowed to have. We would go out for a wonderful Chinese dinner, a movie or a simple errand and on our way home, we'd be accosted by cars with virgin trees tied to their roofs. Our car always had an empty roof.

One evening, as we drove home from Lee's, our favorite Chinese restaurant in Chinatown, it seemed like every car on the road had a Christmas tree slapped onto its rooftop. I couldn't stand it any longer. I blurted, "Dad, please, can't we have a Christmas tree this year. Everyone else has one. Look, we're the only stupid family without one."

"Yeah," said Robert and Michael in unison.

"That's enough," he said. "We are not Christians. We are Jews. We do not celebrate Jesus Christ, the cross or Christmas. Do you hear me? Now, not one more word out of you about a goddam tree."

The saving grace that kept me from being consumed by Christmas envy was the holy, scary manger. It seemed like everyone had one. The grotesquely life-sized mangers scared me the most. Inside the rustic wood house lived a poor sad family with a newborn baby that no one looked happy about. There were too many intrusive and mean looking visitors with their bony animals. The scene didn't look like a celebration of someone's birth.

Despite the terrifying mangers, I loved all the stories of Christmas. My favorite thing to do was to roll myself into a big ball with my blanket on the couch and watch my beloved Christmas movies: A *Charlie Brown Christmas, It's a Wonderful Life* and my all-time favorite, *Miracle on 34th Street*. The movies validated my belief in angels and satisfied my deep longing for happy endings. No matter how difficult their hardships, everyone always came back together and celebrated Christmas.

My other joy was the carolers who came to our door every year with candles in their hands and songs in their hearts. After thinking about it for years, I got up the courage to ask my father if I could go caroling. We were at dinner, my father at his customary spot at the head of the table.

I took a deep breath and blurted, "Dad, can I sing with the carolers this year. I spoke to Mrs. D'Amato, and she said they would love to have me join them."

He put his fork down. Beneath the table, I squeezed my fingers and pinched myself hard. There was a dull silence. My stomach ached. After what seemed like an eternity, he spoke without looking up from his plate. "As long as you don't sing and praise Jesus, I don't see why not."

I couldn't believe my ears. But I composed myself. I knew not to act too excited. "Oh my God, score," I thought. This was my dad who refused to have anything to do with Christmas. My heart raced. I wanted to squeal, but held my breath instead and kept sneaking peeks at him to make sure he was still my dad.

The carolers ranged from 5 to 95 years old. Most lived in or near our neighborhood and attended Holy Name Church. Many were part of the church's choir. Our next door neighbor, Mrs. D'Amato, whom I affectionately called Mrs. Tomato-head due to her bright red hair and a backyard full of summer tomatoes, was both a caroler and a choir member.

The carolers didn't haphazardly get together and go out and sing. They took their singing and caroling seriously. That meant we practiced a lot. For a month, we met every Sunday afternoon and some weekday evenings in either the church basement or at someone's home. Caroling lasted the week leading up to Christmas Eve. As much as I enjoyed singing, I didn't like practicing, even things I loved like skating. I thought if you had a gift, you were supposed to be great at it from the get go. I never understood the concept of discipline.

I knew some of the songs a little and most of them, not at all. The group was patient and never once asked me why a little Jewish girl wanted to go out and sing songs about Christmas.

When we met there was never an abundance of food, if any at all. At every Jewish occasion, there was food, a briss, a funeral, a Bar Mitzvah. I mentioned this to my dad, and he said that was why Goyam women were so skinny.

In the songs, the name of Jesus came up a lot. I didn't want to disobey my father's request. I could have cared less if I sang Jesus' name or not. It seemed to me that this Jesus was a pretty good guy, but still I struggled with how to honor my father's wishes. For weeks, as we rehearsed, I sang Jesus' name every time, not seeing any harm in it. Meanwhile, I spent weeks trying to solve my dilemma.

When the night of caroling arrived, I bundled up in colorful clothes. I made sure that my colors blended, having, since the age of four, had a deep affinity with color and design.

Skiing thermals were the first layer of defense against the frigid night air. Jeans, a plaid pullover shirt and red sweater made up the second layer. The third and most colorful layer consisted of my pink ski parka and pants, my after-ski fur boots, striped mittens in pink, purple and red, a pink and a purple ski hat with an extra-long white wool scarf finished with pink pom poms on the ends. I felt like a colorful stuffed pig.

I walked downstairs to the den where my parents were relaxing and reading. My dad caught a glimpse of me from under his newspaper.

"Oh Ellie, you'll be the best looking caroler they've ever had. Jackie, take a look at your daughter. What a beauty she's become. Come here and give me a kiss," Dad said, shoving his newspaper aside.

I walked over, wrapped my arms around his neck and gave him a kiss on his cheek. "Thanks Dad."

"You're welcome. Now get out there and go have fun. I'll be listening for you."

I practically flew over to the Christianson's, a few doors down. When I entered their home, there was a sea of people dressed up in layers of colorful clothes, coats, hats, mittens, and scarves swarming in their living room. Mrs. Christianson had made a batch of warm chocolate chip cookies and a huge vat of mulled hot cider. The sweet smell of cinnamon effused the room. The fireplace crackled and popped on perfect cue to people's laughter and conversation. Some of the older men in the corner were warming up their throats on pitch. Almost everyone's colors clashed. But together, we blended with a painter's perfection. Mr. Christianson handed everyone a song pamphlet and a candle.

As we walked out into the crisp night, my heart raced. Mrs. D'Amato knocked on the first door. An older woman with white hair in a bun opened the door. We gathered into a tight semi-circle and began to sing, "Away in the Manger." When we came to the word Jesus, I remained silent, smiled and hummed.

"Away in a manger
no crib for his bed
The little Lord mmmm…
Laid down his sweet head
The stars in the heavens
Looked down where he lay
The Little Lord mmmm…

In honor of my father, I sang this way the entire evening. We may not have been permitted a Christmas tree, but as the hefty crystalline snowflakes gently landed on my hat and gloves, I had found where I belonged.

Many Friday nights, we drove a half-hour to Temple services in Boston. At home we didn't keep kosher, but we observed and celebrated all the holidays. We were Reformed Jews. The cultural and historical aspect of being a Jew ran deep in our veins. My parents insisted that we know about our ancestors' history.

We studied the meanings and rituals of each holiday, as well as how to prepare the proper foods. For Rosh Hashanah, we learned to cook down the prunes, sweet potatoes, carrots and cinnamon until it was all mushed together into a puree called tsimmis. At Yom Kippur we learned to fast and reflect on our failings so that we could do better in the year ahead. My Dad taught me how to cook cream cheese filled blintzes and potato latkes for Hanukkah. We all learned to create the Seder plate with salt water, lamb shank, hardboiled egg, celery leaves and horseradish for the bitter herbs. Besides being able to prepare the elaborate dishes of Passover, we also took turns reading from the Haggadah (Passover prayer book), telling the story of Passover as it had been told for thousands of years.

I was also reared in the etiquette of marriage: you must marry a Jew. And yet, at the dating age, I was allowed to date non-Jewish boys or Goyams, as my father called them, as long as they were white. It was clear, however, that these boys would never be acceptable for a husband. Only a Jewish boy would do.

I was always trying to blend in with my Christian friends at school and in our neighborhood, and it was easy to explain our few absences because many of our holidays began at sunset. But when it came to Passover, all bets were off. At Passover, being a Jewish kid, you could no longer hide your difference due to the issue of lunches. Lunches consisted of PB&J matzah sandwiches. Matzah — a board of unleavened bread — could never be disguised as anything else but a foreign, freaky cracker. With every bite, big or small, it crumbled, leaving crumbs and matzah dust everywhere. It commemorated our ancestors, who as slaves in Egypt didn't have time to wait for their bread to rise as they escaped. It was impossible to explain all of this to my Christian schoolmates at lunchtime. Forget it. You might as well just go and sit in the corner with a dunce cap on.

I threw my favorite red checkered lunch box on the kitchen table as I walked in the door. "No more. I'm not eating these stupid sandwiches anymore at school. They're stupid!" I stamped my feet.

"Ellen, it's only a few more days and Passover will be over. Then you'll have your regular sandwiches back again," my mother replied.

"No, don't put those matzah sandwiches in my lunchbox. I won't eat it."

"You need to eat. You can't go all day without eating."

"Yes, I can, and I will. Even if you put it there, I'm not eating it. I'll just throw it in the trash. They're stupid, and I'm not eating it."

"What happened?"

"Nothing. They're just stupid, and they crumble and make a huge mess everywhere. And no one else has to eat those stupid sandwiches."

"Because no one else is Jewish. You are, and you'll eat them," my father yelled from the den.

"No I won't," I yelled back.

"Ellen, watch your mouth," he yelled.

"I'd rather die than eat them at school," I said, stomping up the wooden stairs to my bedroom. "I don't care if I die. I'm not eating them ever again!" I yelled and slammed my bedroom door.

The saddest thing of all was this was one of my favorite Jewish holidays. Passover was one of the happier times in our family. My parents spent an enormous amount of time and energy preparing the food. They cooked brisket, turkey, matzah stuffing and tsimmis. My father always seemed happier and far less explosive, my mother was calmer and more joyous. Together, we sat around the dinner table and celebrated the springtime holiday of release, renewal and rebirth. With each new prayer, we kids drank grape juice while my parents sipped sticky sweet Kosher wine.

I think my parents could have survived my matzah sandwich hysteria, the nuns and even Christmas. The final straw, however, came the day I ran into the house breathless from school and asked my mother what a kike was. I watched my mother's face grow stern and serious.

"Where did you hear that name?"

"Some of the older boys chased me home from the playground yelling, 'Kike, kike, your mother is a kike, kike, kike. You're just a little kike. Hey little kike. Why don't you and your family just take a hike.'"

Her face went pale and sad.

"What?"

"Don't listen to those boys. They're just being stupid little boys."

"Mom, what is a kike?"

"Don't ever say that word again. Do you hear me?"

I knew not to push her, but was confused as to why she was so upset by the word. I assumed it was some kind of a kite. "Yes. I'm sorry."

"It's okay. Go outside and play," she said as tears formed at the corners of her eyes. I went outside, sat under the tree and wondered what the word meant. I could tell it was bad but didn't know why.

A month after the "kike" incident, my dad announced that we were moving to a wonderful new town called Brookline, a place where there were lots of other Jewish families and fabulous schools without nuns.

Brookline was quite different than West Roxbury. The houses were not only larger but also more ornate and lavish. Many dated back to the early 1900's. Almost everyone in our neighborhood was Jewish and far more affluent than the families in West Roxbury. We were no longer the only ones going to Temple on Friday nights. I was amazed to see many of the girls wearing pierced earrings. Some of them even had diamond studs.

The local bakery was run by Jewish women rather than the Irish women I had become accustomed to. Some of them even had concentration camp tattoos. Bagels, challah bread and cinnamon rolls replaced hot cross buns and soda bread.

I liked the old house we moved into, with its quirky details like an ancient intercom system from the early 1900s that allowed you to talk between floors, its diamond shaped windows on the 3rd floor and three bathrooms.

All of our neighbors were Jewish. A rabbi lived next door. That fall, we were invited to celebrate Sukkoth with the doctor who lived across the street. When Christmas arrived, all the other houses on our street remained the same as ours. We were no longer the only unadorned darkened house at Christmas time.

You would think that I would have been sad to leave Christmas and caroling behind, but I wasn't. We'd moved a lot, and I had learned not to miss things or people. By the time we landed in Brookline, we had moved four times. Dad would get behind on the rent or have a fight with the landlord.

Brookline was close to my great grandfather Zayze, a Russian Jew who came alone to America on a boat when he was 14. He had lost his entire family due to the persecution of Jews. His thick white hair stood out against his soft tanned face, deep knowing eyes and a soft plump belly. Although he was a rather small statured man, his heart was as vast and as wide as the Atlantic Ocean. He was truly a king among men.

On Sunday afternoons, we'd often go visit Zayze at his home, which he designed, built and won great acclaim for. To me, it was just my great grandfather's home that smelled of dark, earthy chicken livers. To many in the building industry, however, Zayze's home was considered a revolutionary design of great excellence.

All of the single story houses were connected to each other in a semi-circle. The open space provided all of the tenants with private parking as well as direct access to their individual units. It was one of the earliest concepts of the town homes we are so familiar with today. Zayze never spoke or boasted about his achievements.

One Sunday, shortly after my family arrived at Zayze's and shared our customary greeting of hugs and kisses, Zayze ushered me into his study, while the other kids ransacked his house for candy and my parents read the Sunday paper in the living room. The afternoon sun drenched the small crème colored room through the double-hung windows that encompassed the perimeter of the room. A heavy mahogany desk took up the length of one wall. A comfortable looking crème colored fabric chair sat in one corner, and a daybed sat against the other wall. Zayze and I sat side by side on the daybed with our feet dangling. He had on his customary wool darned socks that were made just for him. In his entire life, he never wore a pair of store-bought socks. I teased him that one day I'd make him wear a pair of "real" socks.

"Oh, Schmeckle," he said using his Yiddish nickname for me, which meant dot, "those regular socks don't feel right to these feet. These ones feel just right for Zayze's toes." I'd never seen his bare feet, but imagined he had long, extra skinny toes that could not be accommodated by the regular American socks.

"You know Schmeckle, people are like feet. Most everyone has a pair and yet feet are so unique. So, we must treat all people with respect and accept their unique way. And in return, they will learn to accept and respect you." He took a deep breath. I smiled at him. There was a pause as he sat thinking. "Schmeckle, no matter how people treat you, you must treat them with kindness."

Usually when he said something like this, I would nod. But today, I couldn't. "But Zayze, what if someone really hurts you or is mean to you or someone you love?!"

"Schmeckle, those are the people you are to love the most. They are the ones who need love the very most."

I hated his answer. Did he know "the people" I was talking about was his own grandson, his own flesh and blood?

"Zayze, why should I be nice to them when they have been mean? They should be hurt so that they can feel what they are doing to others."

Zayze lowered his eyes and shook his head. He seemed to retreat to some faraway place. After a few moments, I was afraid he had died. When he opened his eyes, I saw a deep pain. I wanted to look away. "No Schmeckle," he said, "they will never learn from being hurt or from fighting." He turned his square body to face me and took my small hands into his thick warm ones. "No. You must love them, Schmeckle. Love is the only way. There has been enough pain, enough war, enough killing. Enough. No more."

I put my head down. I couldn't look into Zayze's eyes. In my heart, I knew he was right, but I wanted to be mad, needed to be mad, had a right to be mad. How my father behaved wasn't right. Those boys who yelled kike weren't right. No one, not even Zayze, could have convinced me otherwise. I didn't know what I felt about the boys, but I knew that I loved and hated my father, both at the same time.

As soon as we hopped into the station wagon to go home, my father flew into one of his ballistic tirades for no apparent reason. "Didn't I tell you not to touch the fucking heat," he screamed at my mother in his most blood curdling manner.

Sitting in the back seat on the hump, I heard Zayze's words. "You must love them, Schmeckle. They are the ones who need it the very most." But I couldn't find a way to love the monster driving the car. Instead, I spent the whole ride home hating him, wishing he were dead.

As soon as we were home, I ran to my room on the third floor and pulled out my brown leather journal from in between my bed and the wall. "Dear God, please," I wrote on the thick vanilla page, "you have to get down here and help us. Please. It's getting worse, and I don't know what to do. Please we need you! Love Always, Ellen."

Around the perimeter of my letter to God, I doodled odd, dark faces of men, flowers, swooping circular shapes and hearts. I thought of Zayze's words and wondered if God was up there watching me.

I'd wonder for hours about God. Why would this mighty God, knower and seer of all, let my father hurt us? After what seemed like hours of going in circles in my brain, I concluded two things, either there was no God, or there was something wrong with me. Dismissing the thought that there was no God — I couldn't bear that — I was left with the conclusion that there must be something wrong with me. What was so wrong or bad about me that God didn't think I was worth helping? If I didn't know what to fix about me, I would never get any better.

Some voice in my head politely and expertly explained that since my father was considered a "bad apple" by his own mother, I, being his offspring must also be considered a "bad apple" by everyone, including God. This was the only reasonable explanation. I tried to make sense of my grandmother's hatred of my father, her only son. Unlike most Jewish mothers who smothered and doted on their sons, my grandmother believed boys did not need to be taken care of. Girls, on the other hand, were to be coddled and made into princesses. But even this did not explain my grandmother's hatred toward my father. Her hatred was especially confounding because she was the daughter of my beloved Zayze.

By the time I was 14, I had visited a handful of friend's churches. I wanted to understand as much about God as I could. There was Dixie's Roman Catholic church, Dalia's Lithuanian church, Stephanie's Greek Orthodox church, Kathleen's Catholic church, and DeeDee's black Baptist church. It didn't matter what kind of church it was. I was curious about where everyone went to pray, how they prayed and what their rituals and celebrations were.

My favorite church was St. Ignatius, my best friend Dixie's Roman Catholic church. Points along the roof line made up the soaring arches inside the church. Intricate stained glass windows lined the walls, and high dark wooden pews lined the floor.

"Ellen, let's sit there," Dixie said, taking her seat in an empty row. As I tripped over the kneelers that I always seemed to forget existed, my face turned beet red and hot. I could feel the old ladies' eyes on me. They knew I was Jewish.

"Don't worry," Dixie said in a hushed tone, "You're fine."

I looked at her and rolled my eyes. "You sure?"

"You're fine," she said.

The echo of the footsteps of the priest and the altar boys against the concrete floors shot through my already nervous body like a jolt. I squeezed Dixie's hand. They began chanting, "Deus, in adiutorium meum intende. Domine, ad adiuvandum me festina. Gloria Patri, et Filio, et Spiritui Sancto. Sicut erat in principio, et nunc et semper, et in saecula saeculorum. Amen. Alleluia."

The rhythm and sounds of the Latin chant allowed me to breathe deeper into my high-pitched nervous system. The taut muscles in my body relaxed. My breath deepened and expanded even more as the chant continued. The smell of the old resin in the church reminded me of Zayze's study. The light coming through the stained glass windows took me even deeper into calm. I felt safe. Breathing into and upon the waves of ancient sounds, I could feel God inside of me. He was more real than my father's belt or my mother's desperate drunken cries.

Te deum laudamus: te Dominum confitemur.

Te aeternum Patrem omnis terra veneratur.

Tibi omnes Angeli, tibi Caeli et universae Potestates:

Tibi Cherbubim et Seraphim incessabili voce proclamant:

Sanctus: Sanctus: Sanctus: Dominus Deus Sabaoth

During the midnight mass at Christmas, I had the added excitement and delight of the altar boys swinging sterling silver incense holders that hung from long metal chains. The smoke billowed in thick clouds. Musky frankincense buried itself deep into my long brown hair where I could revisit the scent the next day.

During these services, the candlelight soothed my soul and allowed me to go even deeper into the sounds and rhythms of those ancient Latin hymns. When the hymns concluded, everyone, except me, headed to the front of the church to receive the body of Jesus Christ.

One day, Dixie turned to me and said: "Why don't you go and get one?"

"No." The priest would know I was a Jew.

"Then you'll know what they are like."

"Dixie, look around. Do I look like anyone here?"

"Who cares? Plus you really don't look that strange."

I would not budge. They'd throw me out of the church if they knew I was Jewish.

Dixie was determined for me to know what this wafer tasted like. She went up, stood in line, did the sign of the cross and opened her mouth to receive the body of Christ from the priest. When she returned, she turned to me and took the wafer out of her mouth. "Here, try it."

I put it in my mouth. It was the same wafer as the flying saucers we'd get at the penny candy store, which were filled with white sugar pellets.

"You should have told me, Dix. It's just like the flying saucers."

Dixie's face scrunched up and turned beet red. A bark of a laugh escaped her lips. She slapped her hand to her mouth. Still she couldn't control the laughter. She scooted down the bench, and walked hard and fast toward the door. I followed. As soon as the door slammed behind us, she leaned against the stone building holding her side and let out a huge guffaw. "You can never say that again to me, okay."

"What?"

"Flying…" Again her laughter took hold of her. "I swear I'm going to pee."

I started laughing because of her laughter. "Oh my God."

Dixie pulled a pack of Marlboro's from her handbag and lit one. "Seriously, flying saucers? Oh my God, really?"

I pulled out my pack of Lark's and lit one. "Just what it

seemed like to me."

"Oh my God, Father O'Shannahan would die if he ever knew you said that. Let's go." Dixie stamped out her cigarette on the ground. "Shhh," she said as she opened the heavy wooden door with its Latin numbers intricately carved near the top. "No more jokes, okay?" she said. I nodded and smiled.

I continued to go to church with Dixie on as many Sundays as I was invited. When she was wasn't available, I found other friends to go to church with.

I searched for God everywhere, in all religions, all people and all natural elements. Yet, I struggled to make sense of the contradictions. How could my father love God and hurt us? How could people kill in the name of God? How could most religions think they were the chosen ones or worse, the only ones who knew and fulfilled God's wishes?

As a young thinker and poet, I felt that there was only one God and many different ways to hear his message. By 13, I professed my complete understanding of God to Dixie one day while we sat smoking on the bridge near her church.

"You know, Dix," I said, taking a good hard drag of my Lark, "There should just be one world religion in which all people love God while respecting each other's differences, cultures, and languages. It's just bullshit that they waste all this time thinking they're the only ones. When are they going to get it? Don't they see? There's just one God. And we all find a way to receive the message of God through our religion, be it Roman Catholic, Jewish, Greek Orthodox, Baptist or whatever. It's really that simple. Beyond that, it's all just a bunch of intellectual crap."

Dixie tilted her head, took a drag and said, "Oh Close. Interesting, but it'll never happen."

My stomach sank. I couldn't believe it. Even my best friend

didn't get it. I took a breath. "Dix, it's the only thing that makes sense. It's so stupid to fight over whose God is better. They sound like a bunch of spoiled brats. My God is better than your God, na, na, na, na, na."

"Yeah, yeah, you might have a point, but you'd better go tell it to God. I don't think anyone else is gonna listen."

From the dark recesses of my being, all of my aloneness crept front and center. Besides the tree that sat outside my window, I was certain that no one else could ever understand the crazy world I lived in with my parents and siblings. I felt much older and wiser than most of my peers because I had been forced to grow up too fast. Dixie was one of the few people who understood me. But even with Dixie, I couldn't bring myself to tell her about my family life. Only my tree and God knew everything about me.

In my search to understand how others worshipped, I attended a catechism class with Kathleen after school. I didn't know what Catechism class was when she invited me but thought it would be fun. The class was held by a nun in the basement of a church. The moment I entered, I could feel the serious tone.

"Good afternoon Kathleen," the thin nun said.

"This is my friend…."

"Hi, I said. "I'm Ellen."

The nun didn't even look at me. To Kathleen she said, "You know my rule when you bring an outsider here. Hurry now, we must get started."

Kathleen looked at me nervously, grabbed my hand and took us to the back of the classroom away from the others. We took a seat in the metal chairs with the desks attached. Kathleen slumped deep into the chair. I followed.

Were we sequestering ourselves because the nun somehow knew I was Jewish or did she treat everyone who came to class this way? Kathleen scribbled something on a piece of paper under the desk. Before she could hand it to me, the nun was standing in front of us. She grabbed the note.

"Thank you very much," she said staring at me. She turned her back and crumpled the paper. "Ignorantia iuris non excusat," she said. She raised her hands up high like an orchestral conductor and said, "Students."

Without warning the students, including Kathleen, fled to their feet, crossed themselves and chanted, "Ignorantia iuris non excusat."

I wanted to scream at that rail thin nun, rip her habit off and run out of that classroom. Instead I just sat there. Kathleen had soupy tears running down her face. I knew she was mortified. She mouthed, "I'm sorry."

I squeezed her elbow, shook my head, leaned over and whispered, "Ignoratio."

For the remainder of the hour as she spoke about rules, I sneered at her. "Rules, rules, rules," she repeated over and over as though she were in some kind of trance. "And if they are not followed completely," she told the class, "Then the sinner deserves to be punished."

"Whoa," I thought, "no matter what Kathleen does she doesn't stand a chance. She's gonna get punished."

Unlike Kathleen's catechism class, I adored Dee Dee's black Baptist church. It looked like Kathleen's and Dixie's church from the outside, but from the inside it couldn't have been more different. The choir's soulful gospel music filled my veins with an internal heat I had not felt at any other church or temple. My heart and soul felt held and seen by the round, fecund black women dressed in their colorful outfits and ornate hats. The congregation swayed and sang with full hearts: "God is real. He's real. Glory Halleluiah." The women fanning themselves in the hot sweaty hall made me feel like I was anywhere but home.

I was one of the few white people in the congregation and

the only white kid. I had never seen a minister filled with so much fire and excitement, so much fury. In a black suit and red ruffled shirt stretched over football sized shoulders, he jumped up and down. His left pinky, adorned with a gold ring with a red ruby, snapped and flicked so feverishly throughout the sermon, I worried he'd send the ring right into one of his congregant's faces.

I loved talking back out loud to the minister with the other congregants. My spirit soared with their songs. I swayed to the right as the women sitting near me fanning themselves swayed to the right. And then to the left. Once, a man in front of me jumped to his feet, "Hallelujah Jesus, Hallelujah, Hallelujah," he cried. We all joined in with him. "Hallelujah Jesus. Praise Jesus. Lord have Mercy."

Crunching through the snow in my boots on the way home after the service, I prayed to God for my father not to ask where I had been. I was forbidden to hang out with black people. I prayed I wouldn't have to lie.

Everyone sat at the dinner table, scarfing up my least favorite meal: meatloaf and mashed potatoes. I was grateful I was late.

"Ellen, aren't you going to eat with us?" my father chided.

"I'm not hungry."

"You're never hungry," he said in a somewhat jovial mood.

"You all eat enough for me." I knew I could joke with him tonight.

"I'm so sorry we couldn't make just the right food for you, your highness. Can you send me the meatloaf down this way? Where were you anyway?'

"Hanging out."

"Can I have some more meatloaf?" my brother Robert asked, shooting me a look that said, "I'm covering your ass tonight, you owe me."

"For God's sake, you eating for ya sista, as well?" My father began to get heated.

"Rise up, I say," I shouted, imitating the preacher, desperate to avert my father's mood. "Rise up, young man," I said to my brother.

Michael laughed and joined in. "Ask and ye shall receive."

"Ellen, that's enough," my father's mood was clearly shifting.

"Oh ye of little faith. Rise up yourself."

"Ellen, I'm not kidding, e-nough. Do you hear me? e-nough."

Trapped

"Ellen, get down here!" my father yelled from the den.

I hurried downstairs so he wouldn't go ballistic.

"Look at this mess. This house is a goddam pigsty. Clean it."

"Dad, I didn't do this," I said, picking up an empty bag of Mars Almond candy bars off of the floor. I spied two bowls with Captain Crunch remains glued to the sides and several drinking glasses sitting on the picnic table to the side of the den.

"It doesn't matter how it got this way. It just needs to get cleaned. Do you hear me?"

"Yup," I said under my breath.

"I'm taking your mother to see the doctor," he said, walking from the den to the living room.

My mother had been spiraling downward for weeks. It was just a matter of time before she'd stop taking her meds, if she hadn't already. I was really scared because she seemed lost. She was walking around with glassy eyes in a constant daze. I knew from her crumpled appearance that the only reason she got dressed was because my father expected her to. Otherwise she would've just stayed in bed.

"I'll be back later," he said as he began to walk out the door. "What should I get the kids for dinner?"

"Pizza," I replied quickly, knowing that I wouldn't have to cook that night after cleaning the whole house.

My mother stood in silence by the door. She looked like a ghost of herself. I was afraid to look at her.

"I'll be back later," he yelled and slammed the front door.

I picked up his overflowing ashtray with an orange popsicle stick stuck to it, carried it to the kitchen and emptied it into the garbage under the sink. Gathering up half a dozen drinking glasses, I thought, "Screw you Dad. I'm not your slave." I would've loved to throw them at him or the walls. But I knew what I had to do. I piled up the blankets and pillows strewn all over the den as if it had been hit by a tornado, and collected three pairs of sneakers, two boys jackets, a sweater, a ratty hairbrush and a used cloth hanky and put them in the laundry basket to bring them upstairs to my siblings' bedrooms where they belonged.

Before we moved to Brookline, when I was 11, Dottie, an older black woman, cleaned our house and watched over us when my mother wasn't feeling well. Dottie was always there. I thought of her as a black version of my grandmother whose name was also Dot, short for Dorothy. She was tall, broad and square like my grandmother. She too had eyes not only on the back of her head, but everywhere. If I was doing something bad, she was the one most likely to find me out. There was nothing I could do to pull the wool over her eyes. Through her large hands that were worn like fine leather and her often raised voice, I could always feel her warmth.

"Ellen, you open that door right now," she yelled from the other side of my bedroom door. "I swear to God, I am going to swat you one if you don't open that door."

I had pushed my tall dresser against my door so that I wouldn't get caught smoking my father's Pall Mall cigarettes. Dottie had seen the burnt butts flying out my window and had gone outside and collected them as evidence to show my father.

"I am going to count to ten, and if that door isn't open, I will break it down. You listenin' to me? Ten, nine, eight..."

I pushed the dresser just enough to open the door.

"You smokin' these?" Dottie stood there with a handful of butts. "You better not be smokin' these. You don't think I see them raining down past the dining room window. At 11 years old, my word, what in heaven's name can you be thinking?"

I burst into tears, not because I had been caught, but because I hated disappointing Dottie.

She looked into her butt-filled palm. "Now tell me why such a pretty little girl would go puttin' ugly, dirty things like these into such a beautiful little body. They're nothin' but ugly, and you're nothin' but beautiful. You hear me? Now this time, I'm gonna keep this to myself. But I find you doin' anything like this again, I'll be the first one to tell your father. Do you understand me?"

I nodded.

"Now go and scrub those hands good. Scrub them clean."

One day, just before we moved, Dottie didn't show up. Nothing was ever said about Dottie not coming with us to Brookline. She disappeared before I had the chance to say goodbye. When I realized she was never coming back, I spent a whole day crying, hating her for not telling me and for not saying goodbye.

I became Dottie's replacement. My father never stated this explicitly but it was his unspoken expectation. I suppose he felt that at 12 years old, I was old enough to clean and cook for our entire family when my mother couldn't. It never felt fair. The other kids were hardly ever expected to clean the house. I wouldn't have minded so much if I had gotten paid for my efforts, or if my hard work was ever acknowledged. But to keep the peace, my father's love and admiration, I did what I was told.

I walked to the first floor bathroom to continue my house cleaning. The small sink in the corner was dotted with old toothpaste glued to the edges. The toilet smelled like stale urine. Once the bathroom was done, I ran through the kitchen like a tornado. For some reason, the kitchen was the least offensive place, though the sink smelled like sour milk, and was piled up with encrusted dishes from the night before.

I vacuumed the wall-to-wall rugs on the first floor, but didn't bother with the stairs, just picked up the big fragments and prayed he wouldn't notice. As I was lugging the heavy vacuum up each stair, a piece fell out. "Goddamn it," I said, "I hate you. I wish you'd just fucking leave or die. Who needs you?"

Picking up the mountain of towels in the corner of the second floor bathroom we all shared, I laughed so hard I started crying. Leaning against the cold tiled bathroom wall, I slid down and sat with my legs open. A bunch of the towels landed in the middle of my legs. "Fuck," I said looking at the mess everywhere. Pounding my fists on the towels, I screamed, "Fuck, fuck, fuck." My voice echoed back at me in the tiled bathroom, going right through my body. "I should just leave this stupid house and this stupid asshole father." My stomach sank with the fear of what he would do to my mother and my siblings and what would happen if he ever found me. The only choice was to stay and finish cleaning the stupid house.

I threw the towels in a pile on the landing. In my parents' darkened bedroom, half the bed blankets were on the bed, half on the floor. There was a pile of clothes lying on the chair next to the closet. Some of the doors of my father's dresser were flung open. Damp towels with shredded edges hung off the side of their claw foot bathtub.

I hung up two of his shirts on metal hangers, a pair of my mother's jeans on a wooden pant hanger and two pairs of his trousers on a large trouser hanger in the closet. I collected all the change and ten dollars from his trousers and put it in my own pocket. Two pairs of his socks, my mother's underwear and two pairs of his underwear along with a graying T-shirt were thrown onto the laundry pile on the landing. I pulled the top sheet up from its crumpled position at the bottom of the bed, folded it over and tucked it into the sides of the bed. I fluffed my mother's pillow.

On my father's side of the bed, I bungled his pillow, bent low over it and spit. My spit left a design of tiny dots. Pulling the bedspread up, I tucked it just the way he liked it and stood back and smiled.

People were surprised to learn that I came from a large family with four other siblings: three brothers and a sister. Even as a youngster, when my father introduced us to someone new, he introduced me last, and people would say, "No, really, are you sure she's yours?"

My face was the spitting image of my mother's, but most of the physical similarities ended there. My mother was short, but not tiny. I was the smallest person in my family both in height and in weight, so small my immediate and extended family worried that I would never grow to a normal size. I used to tell people that great things came in small packages. My other siblings were all taller, bigger boned and heavier. They got my father's genes.

My relationship with my siblings was also skewed by the massive responsibility I felt for my family, and my parents' overwhelming demand for attention. As the eldest daughter, I was second mother to my younger siblings, my father's calming influence, and my mother's mother.

When my mother was depressed or institutionalized, I became the second mother especially to my two youngest siblings. In the mornings, I'd go into their rooms, check to see that they were up, and sometimes have to get them out of bed and to the bathroom to shower, brush their teeth and wash their faces. In the kitchen, I'd make them sandwiches: PB& J, turkey or tuna fish. If we were running late, I'd make sure everyone had lunch money, and Jessa and Brian got to school on time. In the afternoons, after walking them home from school, I'd be back in the kitchen boiling broccoli till it wilted and putting it into a large baking pan with mounds of cheddar cheese, milk and fried onion rings on top. This was one of my favorite dishes my mother enjoyed cooking.

For years, I introduced Jessa and Brian as my kids rather than my siblings. I thought of Brian as mine. As soon as my mother walked through the door with him as a newborn wrapped up in his hospital blanket, I said, "Give me him, he's mine."

Our chronological age divided us into two groups: Robert, Michael and I were in one group and the younger kids, Jessa and Brian in another. At times, it even felt like we were in two different families. The younger kids seemed to have it easier. But being our household, nothing was consistent. Every once in a while, even my eldest brother Robert got a break.

One fall evening, a few weeks before Thanksgiving, we all stood in the living room in line with our report cards. Robert, the eldest with his wavy brown hair and stocky build was first in line, then me, Michael, the tall lean string bean, Jessa with her cherubic chubby cheeks and Brian, the youngest and fairest with his shock of dirty blond hair. My father sat on the sofa. One by one, we handed over our report cards for him to review and sign. I stood in line with so much excitement. I had a secret that I had managed to keep to myself.

Robert handed his card to my father. I shuffled my legs back and forth in anticipation. My father looked at Robert's card filled with D's and F's and asked my brother, "Did you do your best?"

He nodded.

"As long as you do your very best that's all I can ask. Keep at it," my father said, rubbing the top of Robert's head.

My brother smiled and walked away.

Excited, I threw my report card at my father. He looked at it and with a blank face said, "An A minus? What happened here?"

I didn't know what to do first: scream, cry or puke. I thought, "What do you mean? Look, I have all A's. What do you mean what happened here?" I was speechless. Hot tears pooled in my eyes. Stunned beyond words, my heart ached. How could he be so nice to my brother and so mean to me? Weren't all A's good enough for him? I grabbed my report card and ran up to my bedroom.

"Ellen, get down here. Get down here right now," he yelled from the couch.

I threw myself on my bed and cried for the rest of the night. Why couldn't he celebrate my amazing report card? He was always trying to keep me in line by telling me I was too big for my britches.

With her permanent flushed cheeks and sweet smile, my younger sister Jessa was the picture of innocence. One day, she begged me to cut her bangs for picture day at school. She wanted her bangs out of her eyes. I agreed that shorter bangs would look good and accentuate her almond-shaped eyes.

"Okay sit here," I said, patting a space on my bed near the table. "You need to sit very still so that I can cut them straight." Playing beauty parlor, like I did with my mom, was one of my favorite things to do.

Jessa smiled, exposing her dimples, and sat up taller and tightened her body. My heart warmed watching her. Even though we were never that close, I loved this little girl. Having to be her "second" mother and responsible for her not only overwhelmed me but stole any possibility of us just being sisters. Once I made it to our bedroom at night, I would escape into my own world, wanting nothing to do with anyone, let alone a little sister whose neediness felt suffocating.

I cut her bangs and stood back. One part was up too high. "Jessa, you need to sit still," I reprimanded her, knowing damn well that I had screwed up.

I squirted her bangs with the water bottle and re-combed them. "Okay, now sit still." Focusing on the other side of her bangs, my hope was to get them to match. I stood back. The bangs were even higher.

"What about I make them a bit choppy rather than straight? I think that will look good, okay?"

"Okay." She had no idea how bad they looked. I cringed looking at her innocent, trusting smile. A picture of her smiling at my Dad flashed across my mind. He always loved to sing her the song, Michelle my Belle by the Beatles. He'd always sing Jessa My Belle, "Sont les mots qui vont tres bien ensemble, tre bien ensemble." And he'd follow it up with, "I love you, I love you, I love you." Jessa beamed every time he sang her the song. We started calling her Jessa, My Belle and would sing the French to the best of our ability. We never knew what it meant. I always thought it was French for "I love you".

I took another stab at her bangs. I cut them lengthwise as I had seen other hairstylists do and stepped back. They were now even worse. I was horrified but kept a straight face.

"Jessa, still."

"I am."

"Then don't breathe."

Her eyes filled with big pools of tears.

"Ellen, Jessa," my mother yelled, "Where are you guys?"

"Up here," I called.

As my mother walked into my bedroom, she gasped. "Ellen, for God's sake, what did you do?"

I shrugged. "She wanted them done."

Jessa got up and looked in the mirror. She burst in tears. "You've ruined my pictures."

"I'm sorry. I tried really hard to get them straight, honestly."

"Till I had none to straighten," she said, pulling at the pieces of hair that were left of her bangs.

"I could try taping them together." She laughed and cried at the same time. I yanked on them. "Maybe I can make them grow."

"Ellen, what were you thinking?" my mother asked.

"I just kept trying to even them out."

"Well, there's only one thing to do," my mother said.

"What?" said my sister and I in unison.

"Take a picture." She motioned us, and we followed her downstairs. She grabbed the camera out of the front hall closet. We laughed, cried and took pictures of Jessa, sans bangs, smiling for the camera.

Years later, my mom told me why I was conceived. Her mother had recently died and she was feeling depressed. My father took her to see the doctor. The doctor's advice to my father was to get her pregnant. I laughed when my mother told me this.

"Seriously," I said. Could a doctor be that stupid? "What about just grieving?"

My mother looked at me with a straight face. "No, in those days, the doctor thought getting pregnant was always the answer."

Pregnancy hormones did make her happy for nine months. But she was back to square one, feeling depressed, once she delivered the baby. The pregnancy hormones were why she had so many kids.

"I always loved being pregnant," she said. "I felt so good pregnant. And," she went on, "As an only child, I had always wanted to have lots of brothers and sisters."

My stomach sank. "Yeah," I thought, "but we were supposed to be your kids, not your brothers and sisters."

"Ma! Ma!" Michael screamed at the top of his lungs from the landing on the second floor. "Ma, where the fuck are my pants? I need my pants for school. Didn't you wash my pants?"

"I forgot," my mother said meekly as she came up to the landing. "I'm sorry. Don't you have another pair of pants to wear to school today? I'll clean them by the time you get home from school."

"You fucking asshole. How could you fucking forget?"

"Michael, there's nothing I can do right now."

"You fucking asshole. I hate you!"

My mother turned and began walking back down the stairs to the kitchen.

"I hate you." He lunged at her back with his hands and shoved her. She stumbled. "I wish you were dead."

"Lenny," she screamed for my father.

"Michael, enough," he yelled from his bedroom.

My brother stormed back to his room, slammed the door and yelled from behind the door, "Ma, I hate you."

As much as Michael professed to hate my mother, he continued to be my compadre in protecting her from my father. Violent scenes like the orange juice can incident were a regular occurrence. Outside the battle zone, however, my brother's rage often exploded in indecent rants at my mother.

His temper was also aimed at his teachers. He was so emotionally abusive they tried to throw him out of the John D. Runkle School when he was in the sixth grade. My parents refused to let them and promised to get him under control. They never did.

When he was 13, my brother's world collapsed. In one month, he lost thirty pounds. He could hardly tolerate any food or drink, vomited constantly and had putrid smelling diarrhea and farts that stung your eyes. Overnight, he went from being a fat football player to a weak, lanky string bean. Dark purple circles under his hollowed eyes screamed of sadness and death. His clothes hung off of him as though he were living in a concentration camp. He was diagnosed with Ileitis, a disease which caused his colon to become inflamed.

The diagnosis was not the worst part of the ordeal.

One day as my sunken brother walked to his bedroom after his doctor's appointment, I followed him and stood over him as he lay on top of his bed. "What did they say?"

"They said I have Ileitus." He laced his long fingers together.

"And?"

"And the doctor said I'll die young."

"What? What did he really say?"

Imitating the doctor's low voice, Michael said, "Many people with your disease at this level have compromised lives, often living only into their mid to late forties and fifties."

"Well, that doesn't mean *you're* going to die young. What a stupid thing to say anyway."

"Ellen, do the math. He wouldn't have said it if it wasn't the truth." He turned away and stared out at the window. "You just have to face facts."

Why the hell would a doctor ever give a kid at age 13 this information? Didn't he understand how strong the mind is at fulfilling prophecies?

My aggressive, boisterous brother retreated deep into the unspoken recesses of his mind, alone. From my third-floor bedroom, I monitored his illness. I knew if he was having a bad day or an attack by how often I heard his heavy flat footed march to the bathroom. The putrid, acidic smell of his stomach wafted its way through the house.

As Michael moaned on the cold tiled floor in the bathroom, I walked down from the third floor and stood outside the door.

"Michael, you okay?" I could hear him trying to muffle his moan. "Can I come in?"

"No. Leave me alone."

As he vomited, the noise echoed through me. Slumped on the opposite side of the door, I covered my mouth with my right hand and held my stomach with my left. "Michael, can I help you?"

"Go away," he said with a little less edge this time.

I traced the door with my finger lightly. When he flushed the toilet, I got up, walked upstairs, threw myself on the bed and felt hot tears rushing down the sides of my cheek. The house was full of silence.

My brother's disease came and went in fits and spurts. He had to give up football because he was too weak to play. He never seemed to mind that. Regular doses of Prednisone became a way of life to curtail his stomach attacks. He was supposed to adjust his diet, but he never did. And he often suffered the ill effects of Chinese food, pizza or other spicy foods.

One day as my brother was resting on top of his bed after school, I walked into his bedroom and said, "How are you feeling?"

He rolled his eyes and turned his mouth upward and to the left, imitating Jerry Lewis and mimicked me, "How are you feeling?" He maneuvered his lanky body and turned himself into a pretzel. "What do you think sista? Hurry, take my temperature. Do you think I'm going to live?" This became the way he dealt with most things from this point forward. You hardly ever got a straight answer out of him.

Michael wasn't the only one to employ humor as a coping mechanism. Humor played a large role in our family. It was a safety valve where a lot of emotional steam was released. It was one of the saving graces of our life.

One Saturday afternoon when I was 15, I got it into my head that it would be funny for all of us to get into one pair of my father's size 5X pants. Being a teenager, I didn't quite think through the logistics. All five of us climbed inside my Dad's pants at the top of the staircase and started hopping together down the stairs. Halfway down, we started laughing so hard, we lost control and stumbled and tumbled over each other. Michael dropped a bomb. It was hard to tell what was funnier, falling down the stairs together stuffed into our father's pants or Michael's silent but deadly fart. Dad came to find us five in a snorting pig pile. We found the composure to stand up and show him what we looked like in his pants. You could never be sure of Dad's reaction. On this occasion, he laughed so hard his belly shook as though a huge wave was moving through it.

Most events in our household didn't end in laughter, though. One of the worst incidents took place right outside of our house. It was a crisp New England fall day. I heard screaming from outside my bedroom window. It was rare to hear screaming outside our house. Most everything took place behind closed doors as image was so important to my father. My father was screaming at my brother Robert. As the eldest child and the one least likely to fight back, Robert suffered the worst beatings of any of us. I think his refusal to fight back incensed my father. Robert just didn't seem to have the fighter mentality. Perhaps he realized that fighting with a lunatic was senseless. He learned to cope by running and hiding when my father went ballistic.

I ran down two flights of stairs and out the front door. My father had managed to get my brother sandwiched between the curb and the tire of his car. He stood in full view of the neighbors screaming and kicking my brother.

"You fucking asshole. Who the fuck do you think you are?" he screamed, as he kicked him again and again.

"Dad, stop it," I yelled. My brother was face down on the road. "Stop it." He didn't pay any attention.

"Fuck you," he screamed as he kicked. Robert didn't move. His inability to fight back incensed my father to the brink of insanity.

I threw myself in front of him, waving my arms. "*Stop it.* What the fuck are you doing?"

"Get out of my way. Swear to God, Ellen. Get the fuck out of my way."

"Robert, *go*," I yelled.

"If you don't get out of my way…"

"What, you're going to kill me? What? You're going to kill him?"

Robert managed to get up. His nose was covered in blood. As he opened his mouth to say something, his mouth was filled with blood.

"Pussy," he screamed at my father as he ran down the street crying.

I ran after him, into Dean Park behind our house. The trolley track separated the park from our house giving us enough distance from my father. He wouldn't come after us, but I didn't know what he'd do to us once we got home.

Robert ran to the benches by the trees. He put his head in his hands. "I'm not going back, Ellen. I can't. He's fucking crazy."

"I know but what are you going to do? You need to come back. Robert, let me see your face. It'll be alright. He just went crazy."

"I'm sick of it. I just can't go back." He sobbed harder.

"You're right. He's crazy, but you can't live in the park. Please come back. It'll be worse if you don't. It'll be worse for all of us if you don't come back. Please Robert, please come home."

"I can't stand him."

He sobbed with such an intensity I knew my brother's heart was broken. My heart ached for him. We had always been super close as little kids. We'd have arm wrestling matches for hours, give each other Indian rubs until we laughed so hard we cried Uncle. We'd play Operation until our parents took the game away. It wasn't until middle school that we stopped being so close. I hated that he wouldn't fight back, hated that kids called him Porky and made fun of him behind his back, hated that I couldn't do anything at all to change any of it.

I never knew what sparked this incident, perhaps a report card splattered in bold red D's and F's. Like everything else with my father, one moment he could be extremely generous and the next a raging maniac. But it could have been just about anything.

My brother cried for the next couple of hours while I begged him to come home. Where would he go if he didn't come home? In the end, we walked back together in the dark. I prayed my father had gone to his bedroom as he often did after one of his rages.

As we approached the house, the light of the television illuminated my father's figure in the darkened den. I imagined him sitting there with a bag of candy nestled next to him. It would be safe to go inside the house.

Robert and I started up the stairs when my father yelled, "Ellen, get down here."

I whispered, "Go to your room." My brother's eyes looked frightened. "I'll be fine," I said with false confidence, and walked quickly to the den so my father wouldn't get pissed off.

"Get in there and clean the fucking kitchen."

Without a word, I walked into the kitchen and saw the sink full of dirty dishes. "Big fucking deal," I said to myself. "You big baby," I screamed at him in my head. "You're nothing but a big giant baby elephant." I cracked myself up at the image of my father's face connected to an elephant body. I knew better than to laugh and scrubbed the dishes furiously instead. Before I finished, he turned off the TV and went upstairs to his bedroom and slammed the door. I was safe. My brother would also be safe, at least for tonight.

Voice

"Slim often got stuck in the keyhole. This worried his parents for Slim was coming of age and would soon need to go to school. He not only needed to learn how to shrink to fit through keyholes, but also how to hide his full size outside the home. They wanted him to fit in with the other kids at school. Slim didn't want to pretend to fit in, so he never fully applied himself to these lessons."

For weeks I labored over constructing the short story for Mr. Tipton's sophomore creative writing class. The Tall Family had to bend, stretch and contort their bodies to fit into the small house that they lived in between the walls of another family's home.

"On the other side of the keyhole, Slim watched the family's five children — three boys and two girls — play, wrestle and argue. He longed to have siblings. In his head, he'd always take sides with whomever had a better point of view, sending that person thoughts on how to strengthen their argument. He realized, however, that these kids didn't have the telepathic powers that he and his parents possessed. He wished they would notice him through the keyhole and welcome him into their family."

I received my story back on the Tall family. Mr. Tipton wrote in his infamous red oil crayon: "Amazing! A+. Quite accomplished!"

I flew home, ran into the kitchen. My mom sat at the table with a cup of coffee. My dad mixed something in an oversized restaurant metal bowl.

"Look," I said. "I'm destined to be a famous writer."

"And what makes you think that, Hemingway?" My father chuckled without lifting his eyes.

"Dad, look. Mr. Tipton thinks I'm an accomplished writer. Look."

"Ellen, do you know how many people write books and never get published or worse, they sit in a dark room drunk and dejected because their bullshit never got published. Forget about whatever good ole Mr. Tiptoes has to say. There's no future in writing. It's almost as bad as being a musician."

"His name is Mr. Tipton."

"Tiptoes, Lipton, Lipshit. You and hundreds of would-be writers can line up together at the unemployment line with all of your teacher's accolades in hand without a pot to piss in. I don't know why they fill your head with such shit. You need a real profession, Ellen, just remember that. Writing will never pay the bills."

"Daaad."

"Ellen, enough. I have a surprise for dinner."

"I'm not hungry."

"Well you better get hungry."

I ran to my room, fell onto my bed, grabbed my once stuffed brown bear, now deflated from years of leaning on him, and burst into tears. I wished Mr. Tipton had been there to argue with my father. I knew now that I could never be a writer no matter how much I loved it and Mr. Tipton's words.

I stared at the ceiling, seething.

My father didn't deserve to live. I didn't care what Zayze said. I wished he would die. Drop dead of a heart attack. I wished I had the guts to kill him. My siblings could hold him down while I beat him until he couldn't breathe. Or I could give him electroshock therapy and watch him sizzle. My mind ran wild. I knew the power of one's imagination and feared my thoughts could do real harm. Scattered and out of control, I couldn't rein myself in. Shaking, I got out of bed and pushed the dresser in front of my door.

"Oh God, please take my thoughts away. I'm scared. What if I wake up and he's dead? Oh, God. What if I fall asleep and kill him in my sleep? Michael walks in his sleep and never remembers it. Oh God. There are sharp knives in the kitchen. God, sorry, I don't mean these things. I don't know what to do. If you have to, take my left eye, but please leave me one eye. Please let me have my legs. I need my legs. I suppose I could live without one arm. Please don't let me do anything bad in my sleep tonight."

I would never forget my first e e cummings poem. My heart pounded as I read it.

because it's

because it's

Spring
thingS

dare to do people

(& not
the other way

round)because it

's A
pril

Lives lead their own

persons(in
stead

of everybodyelse's)but

what's wholly
marvellous my

Darling

is that you &
i are more than you

& i(be

ca
us

e It's we)

e e cummings

It was as if I were looking in the mirror at my real self, the self buried under a mountain of polite, appropriate, good-girl behavior. The words gave me permission for the way I actually thought.

Cummings screwed with every rule, every axiom of the English language. What looked like a scattering of words was bound by a new structure. His unique but organized way of thinking made more sense to me than traditional structures. I felt a deep alignment with him. He wasn't worried about what people thought. He had the courage to express his uniqueness even though he probably knew it would piss a lot of people off. Without pretenses, he embraced his unusual voice and exploded it onto the page. No apologies. No excuses. I wanted to be like him, to bare my soul, to not dress up my thoughts.

In reading his work, I felt normal and understood. I no longer worried about the Tall family story being too bizarre. I knew what lay beyond the cracks in the wall and wanted to give voice to that. Cummings inspired me to rebel, to express in writing my anger and hurt, as well as my love, words I would not have otherwise dared to say out loud.

I wrote poems in the manner of e e cummings, painted wordscapes across barren pages of my journal. No longer worried about proper etiquette, I emptied my heart and soul. In the imaginative world, I felt safe to use my voice. I had conversations with e e cummings in my head and no longer felt so alone. He comforted my soul. In honor of my hero and friend, I did my senior thesis on him.

We were required to read other writers, but there were only a few that had the kind of impact that e e cummings had. Sylvia Plath also left quite an impression on me.

Plath was a woman who dared to reveal the depths of the darkness that I knew too well. Through *The Bell Jar*, I found a woman who understood my loneliness. I idolized her and would have given anything to be as talented as she was.

After a few months of reading and rereading her poetry and *The Bell Jar*, I began to descend too far into the darkness. I feared I would be swallowed up by the gloom that eventually made her commit suicide. I pushed her books into the back of my closet for safekeeping. To remain sane each day, I needed to keep a smile on my face.

As I walked through the high school quadrangle, I spotted Ms. Learner eating lunch with a stack of papers sitting next to her. She taught the classics, poetry and Shakespearean studies. A cool, unusual teacher, she managed to get the best out of all of us, expecting us to think for ourselves. Through Ms. Learner, I gleaned that there were adults who truly wanted to hear our voices.

"Do you have a minute?" I asked.

"Always, have a seat." She moved her papers to the other side of the bench. "What's on your mind?"

"Sylvia Plath. Do you think that she committed suicide because she spent too much time thinking about the dark places?"

"I don't think she committed suicide just because she contemplated the darkness in humanity. Perhaps her humanity was filled with so much darkness that she couldn't escape it."

"Like what?"

"Like not having the skills to deal with her darkness or a way to balance it with joy."

"Huh. Thank God, I can laugh at a lot of things. But it is kind of creepy thinking about her."

"Yes, her death was very sad, very dark. She definitely lost her balance. I don't think she could see a way out."

"But there's always a way." My life depended on remaining positive. "Have you ever felt like there's no way out?"

"There have been a few times in my life, but I have reminders like my son to show me that there is always a way through things in life." She put her long thin hand over mine. We sat in silence.

There was so much more I wanted to tell her but didn't dare: how Mom battled the darkness, how she screamed at people I couldn't see, how scared I was of getting her disease.

I remained silent. It was too terrifying to think about, let alone talk about.

"Yeah, but at which point does the darkness overwhelm people like Sylvia?"

"That's a very good question. I'm not sure I have a good answer for you. I truly wish I had an answer for that."

Ms. Learner spearheaded SWS (School Within a School) at my high school. I longed to be a part of SWS, but it required a parent's signature. I spent a month copying my father's signature during 10th grade. I decided against using it. Forging his signature could only result in serious trouble. Behind his back, I did manage to take one of Ms. Learner's SWS classes. It was one of the most rigorous, thought-provoking classes of my high school education. In her presence, I felt a non-judgmental loving space where I was free to explore the truth of my dark spaces through written and spoken voice.

> My mistress' eyes are nothing like the sun;
> Coral is far more red than her lips' red,
> If snow be white, why then her breasts are dun;
> If hairs be wires, black wires grow on her head.

"Ah, there my friends," Ms. Learner exploded with excitement as she paced in long giraffe-like strides around the edge of our circle of chairs. We were studying Shakespeare, reading, exploring and creating our own sonnets. Sitting in an overstuffed yellow chair toward the front of the classroom, I wished my mother could be like Ms. Learner, elegant, bold, outspoken and powerful.

"There, do you see what he's done," she said. "He just turned it all around on us in a split second. So, what is he saying?" Her auburn hair flew with as much buoyancy as if she were swinging in the park.

"He's saying, 'I love you even though you're not the kind

of pretty we'd expect my mistress to be for me to love her,'" I answered.

"Lovely, Ellen, lovely."

> I have seen roses damask'd, red and white,
> But no such roses see I in her cheeks;
> And in some perfumes is there more delight
> Than in the breath that from my mistress reeks.

"Can you imagine," she said, her words elongated in a slight southern twang, "a man loving you this much and with such a good sense of humor?" She stretched her long body forward for emphasis. "James, tell me what do you think he was saying, when he wrote: I love to hear her speak, yet well I know/That music hath a far more pleasing sound?"

"James, are you with us today?" James sat in the corner in an oversized chair half asleep. "James, dare I interrupt your silence that doth not become you?"

The class cracked up.

"I grant I never saw a goddess go," James answered in a lazy voice.

"Aha, you are here. Thank you, Mr. James."

> My mistress, when she walks, treads on the ground:
> And yet, by heaven, I think my love as rare
> As any she belied with false compare.

Ms. Learner took a deep breath. "That, my friends, is pure genius. Thanks to Ms. Close, we will soon have a new modern version of this sonnet next week. How's that going?"

"It'll go better now that I have sat through this. Thanks."

"We look forward to your sonnet next week." She smiled broadly. "Ok, now for the pièce de résistance of the day. Wendy will present her chosen sonnet. Wendy, it's all yours."

We gave our final presentations at Ms. Learner's home in Cambridge. She served freshly baked lemon cookies, scones, a rich chocolate molten cake, fruit and a sparkling drink served in champagne flutes. We recited our sonnets in her sun-drenched living room enclosed with French doors while Mozart played in the background.

At the beginning of my senior year, I was sitting watching MASH. My father tore into the den and stood in front of the TV. "Mr. Roberts called me today and informed me that you'll soon be done with your high school requirements. What are your plans?"

This was the first I had heard anything about finishing my credits early. I tried to see around him to watch the ending of the show. "I don't know."

"Well, let me give you an idea." He was getting agitated. "There's the door, or there's college."

My heart and stomach sank. Had he just threatened to throw me out on the street? Accustomed to him threatening to throw my mother out, I never imagined he would do it to me. I stared at him, my eyes filling with hot, stinging tears. "Fine then, college."

"Enough screwing around now, Ellen. Get busy and go find one to go to. You don't have much time. Do you hear me?"

I walked up to my bedroom in shock. I had just been thrown away like useless garbage. There had been no prepara-tion. That was it. "Fuck," I thought, rolling the conversation around in my brain, trying to make some sense of it. He acted like I had hidden this information from him.

I walked back downstairs. "Dad." I knew I was walking on thin ice. "Why are you so mad? I didn't lie to you."

"Ellen, enough. You don't have any fucking time to waste. Go find a fucking college to go to."

I wanted to run to my mother, but knew she would take

his side. She always took his side. She'd even crawl into bed with him after a night of verbal battering. It disgusted me and made me crazy. Why didn't she fight back? Instead, she'd go silent, bow her head and obey. I wanted to scream for both of us, but there was no sound.

Secrets

The sun shone upon the crisp leaves scattered in varying hues of bright and golden yellows, burnt oranges and reds. It was a flawless New England fall day. I grabbed a rusted rake leaning against the dilapidated garage, and made a pile against the backside of our old wood house.

In the old garage that no one ever set foot in, I discovered five-foot planks of wood. I dragged three of them out, hoisted them on top of the leaves and formed a triangle. When I lit a few matches and threw them onto the pile, the crisp leaves burst into flames, setting the wood on fire. My heart raced.

One flame led to another until the fire grew higher than me. A plank collapsed, standing like a pole in the leaves, and the flames danced around it. My body both raced with excitement and seemed to relax. I was mesmerized by the amber flames dancing around the pole. Another piece of wood fell in the direction of the house. Sparks and flames shot toward the house's back wall.

"What is wrong with you?" my father screamed as I sat on the crushed blue velvet sofa in the den.

I shrugged, unable to remember what happened between setting the fire, and ending up in the den with my father. Obviously, my father had extinguished it. I could smell the smoldering leaves and wood.

"Honest to God, Ellen, one more fire anywhere and you are going to juvey. And I will not come and get you. Mark my words. Do you hear me? What in the hell is wrong with you? Do you think it's funny to be a pyromaniac? Only mentally ill people light fires. What's wrong with you? You could have set this entire house on fire. You're just damn lucky you didn't."

I spied his green glass ashtray that looked like a shell sitting on the side table. It was filled with the remnants of my fire experiments: matches, sticks and cigarettes.

It all began a few months earlier after school one day. No one was home. Sitting on the sofa just staring out the window, I decided to line up matches on the bottom of the ashtray and set them on fire. Watching the flames take off and then die out, was mesmerizing and strangely calming. Over time, I built more elaborate fires in the ashtray, adding strips of paper towels, toilet paper, torn pages of notebook paper and popsicle sticks. Each day, I spent more time thinking about fire and coming up with extravagant ways to build them until it culminated with my experiment outdoors, by far my largest fire.

I was grounded for a month. The grounding didn't bother me as much as not being able to make fires. I smoked more Larks and had to be satisfied watching the cigarettes burn down.

Fires were one secret. There were others: the violence in our house, my mother's crazy drinking, my father's arrest (handcuffed and thrown into the back of the paddy wagon in the middle of the night), smoking cigarettes, my crazy thoughts, how much I loved writing, having the lights and phone shut off, finding boxes filled with porn tapes in the attic, my father's interrogation by the FBI, how afraid I was of people finding everything out, my father having a girlfriend, finding a gun in the closet, our family being threatened by a guy to whom my father owed money.

Even at school, I hid the facts, and discovered early on that the school authorities wouldn't believe me anyway. During 6th grade, I went to the counselor's office one morning after a horrific night of my parents' fighting. She showed me a box of dolls. I took a male doll and a female doll and showed her exactly how my father hit my mother, and how my mother cowered. After I stopped crying hysterically, she asked me if I wanted to stay in her office or go back to class. I chose to go back to class. I liked school. It was one of my safe places.

I didn't know who the counselor spoke to, or how the decision was made, but the next day I was placed in a speech class with kids who had lisps, stutters or were mildly retarded. There was nothing wrong with my speech. The only thing I could surmise was the school must have called my father and told him what I said. He, in his charming manipulative manner, must have said something like, "Oh, you know that Ellen. She's a great storyteller." I imagined that he suggested the speech class as punishment. There was no other sane way to explain it. I didn't dare ask. From then on, I didn't tell anyone in authority what went on behind closed doors. Speech class was one thing to have to bear, an asylum or prison was quite another. It wasn't until I met Ms. Learner in high school that I dared to share some of what went on in our house.

I met Danny the summer I was 13, while my family was vacationing on Cape Cod. His sister did charcoals on Main Street to make money. He was standing at her stall when I walked up to look. Her pictures were sculptural and captured people's essence. There was a picture of Danny that caught his bigger than life presence — his large chiseled nose set against devilish green eyes and thick black hair that hung to his shoulders that he got from being part Cherokee. I liked him immediately. He was older and probably too tall at 6 feet 6 inches.

"Are you new here?" he asked.

"I'm here for the summer."

"Where are you staying?"

"We have a house in Centerville."

"Well, if you get bored, a bunch of us meet here at night and play music over there in the basement of the church. Maybe you can come sometime."

"Yeah, maybe."

"I'm Danny Dachel, and this is my gifted sister Arlene."

"Hi, I'm Ellen. Nice to meet you both. I gotta go," I said and began to walk away.

"We meet over there," he said, pointing to the gazebo on the lawn. 7:30ish. Come some night. See you soon." He winked at me.

"Later." My heart soared and then fell. I'd never felt anything like this before. Would I ever see Danny Dachel again?

I managed to convince my parents to keep coming back to Main Street, secretly hoping to run into Danny. It didn't take long. My parents liked him immediately and began to allow me to go meet him and his friends at night even though he was 16.

Danny's family was artistic and unusual. Arlene drew, painted and did charcoals. His brother, Martin, was a genius inventor and played around with electronics, read a lot and was always working on equations. His mother was artistic and owned a candle shop. She was the person responsible for supporting the family. I couldn't believe that a mother could run her own store and support her family. She was obese; she was as fat as my father. I figured since she wasn't pretty, it was okay for her to be powerful.

His father was always off hunting. I never really knew what he did other than stay away from his mother. Danny told me that when his father was there, there was so much tension he was always relieved to see him go, even though he always seemed to miss him. His parents stayed married for some reason I never understood.

I loved being around Danny's family. My parents would let me take the Greyhound bus from Boston to the Cape and stay with Danny and his family on weekends throughout the school year. His mom adored me and was always happy to see me. His sister and brother inspired me. In their presence, I felt normal. My ideas and imagination didn't seem out of the ordinary. No one ever shot me down or called me names.

Danny was an amazing potter, creating pieces good enough to compete with well-known adult potters. He made miniatures for me. I couldn't imagine how his long fingers were able to create a pot the size of my thumb. He won many awards, including "Most Promising Young Artist" from some national art council.

Danny and I spent hours imagining ourselves as artists. He, a famous potter and me, a famous writer like e e cummings. As we dreamed together, we'd trace on each other's arms with our fingertips. All the chaos, violence and fear of my house seemed to slip away. I felt free.

"You know, you're just like Oblio," he said, running his fingers through my hair.

"Yeah, how's that?"

"You're one of a kind. And I have a feeling that you'll show them all one day some very good points just like Oblio. I hope I'm there."

I smiled.

Danny lit up a joint, took a drag and passed it to me. I took a hit and held it deep in my lungs.

Oblio was the main character of Harry Nilsson's story, "The Point." Danny and I listened to it on his record player dozens of times. Oblio was the only round-headed person in the Land of Point where, by law, everyone and everything had to have a point. Eventually, the evil Count banished Oblio to the pointless Forest, even though he was beloved by many, including the King. But even in the pointless forest he found that everything had a point. He returned to the Land of Point and taught the people that everyone, including him, had a point and purpose. The evil Count, having heard enough, ripped Oblio's hat off to reveal a point atop his bare head. Suddenly, the points of everyone and everything began to disappear. Oblio was welcomed home and celebrated. I cried each time I got to the ending of this story. I longed to feel that kind of acceptance.

I put my head in Danny's lap and breathed. In his presence I always felt protected, and dreaded having to go back home.

Even with Danny I had to keep secrets. I'd remind myself: Don't tell Danny too much about my father; don't tell anyone how much I loved Danny, don't tell my girlfriends about sex—how much I knew and how much I liked it. Don't speak about the make-out parties, smoking pot, and trying Opium and loving it. Don't tell anyone about going with Gloria for her late stage abortion.

"Is that too tight?" I asked Susan as she sat in front of me in the braiding circle with Beth and Nicole. We sat in Susan's bedroom as we had on so many Saturday nights, feasting on junk food and gossiping. Her room was filled with matching white furniture fit for a little girl. One of the matching beds had a white canopy above it. I wished I had such a perfect girl's room.

"No, it feels just right, perfectly tight," Susan answered.

I braided her wet hair into tiny braids down the middle of her back. My mind swirled with my father's latest explosion at my mother just a few hours earlier.

"You fuckin' bitch," he screamed in the den. "When the

fuck are you going to get your fucking head examined? I should just throw you out onto the fuckin' street. You're as good as a goddamn whore."

"Please Mom," I prayed, "scream, fight back."

My mother stood there with her head down and her shoulders rounded, never saying a word. He left the den, went up to their bedroom and slammed the door so hard I thought it would come off of its hinges.

Susan snapped a small rubber band on my leg. "Hello? Earth to Ellen, come in. Are you there?"

"Yes, commander," I muttered.

My mother lowered herself to the crushed blue velvet couch, steadying herself on her left arm and folding her legs underneath her. Without seeming to notice me, she pulled a pack of Salems from the pocket of her jeans and lit one. Tears slid out the corner of her eyes. She grabbed the large green glass ashtray from the side table and twirled her cigarette, rolling the ashes off of it. I bent and placed my hand on her back. She pulled away. "Go to Susan's. I'll be okay."

"Mom, I don't need to go. We're just going to be sitting around braiding hair."

"I'm okay." She dragged hard on her cigarette.

"Why don't you leave him?"

"Ellen, go."

"Okay, but you promise to call me if he does anything more, right?"

"Ellen, it'll be fine. Go. Have fun."

I walked to the front door. My father stood there. "Remember," he said, "nothing ever goes on here." I grabbed the door handle. He put his hand over mine. "Tell me."

"Nothing ever goes on here," I parroted back.

"Just remember that."

"Ellen, do you have a rubber band?" Beth asked, holding a freshly made braid of Nicole's hair.

I jumped, startled. Everyone laughed.

"Jumpy, jumpy, jumpy," Nicole said. "What's the matter, you see a ghost?"

Susan and Beth giggled.

"I hear Close thinks there's a ghost that lives in her attic. True?" chided Nicole, re-doing one of her braids.

"Well, if you must know," I said with aristocratic arrogance. "There is indeed a ghost who lives in the attic. His name is Alfred. He's a smart, friendly ghost who thinks that you stink because you knock ghosts."

I was trying to hide the fear, shame and rage boiling within me about my parents. I was also trying to hide what I knew about ghosts, demons and angels. I was certain that most people didn't have angel visitations, or talk with God on a daily basis. I was petrified to tell anyone, let alone these girls, about my contact with angel beings. They were too close to my mother's dreams. If I wasn't careful, I'd go crazy like my mother. When the girls or anyone else made fun of ghosts or angels, I played along.

"Really? What do you know about ghosts anyway?" Nicole asked.

"Wouldn't you love to know?" I said, grabbing a handful of pretzels.

"I can't imagine," Nicole said. "There isn't anything we don't already know."

My chest tightened. I would have loved to spill the beans about everything, the angels, my father's rages, but whatever I said to Nicole would go back to her mother and then to my father as they were good friends.

"Anyone up for truth or dare?" Nicole asked, finishing off the bag of potato chips she took from Susan's kitchen. "Ow," Nicole squealed. "That's too tight."

"OK, Ellen, truth or dare?"

"Truth," I lied.

"How far have you gone with Danny?"

"If you must know, we have kissed." I wasn't about to tell them that we'd had make-out sessions for hours, that I allowed him to go to second base or that we smoked pot.

"When do we get to meet him?" Susan asked, sitting cross-legged like her parents who meditated.

"Sometime. When he's up here, but that's not that often 'cause he uses his mother's van to come up, but she usually needs the van for the store she runs."

"God, you sound married to him for God's sake. Are you going to marry him?" Nicole asked.

"Who knows, but it wouldn't be for a really long time. I'm in no rush. I don't really even know if I ever want to get married. Do you?" I asked Nicole.

"Yeah, but not like my mother. I actually want it to last forever."

"That would be nice, if it's right, but otherwise you should just leave."

"Seriously, you would just leave, really?" asked Nicole.

"Yup. Absolutely."

"You sound so certain. How do you know what you'd do?"

"I just know," I said. Nicole cocked her head to the left and looked at me as if she didn't believe me. "Promise, I know," I assured her.

Two weeks later, it was my turn to have the girls over. I never knew what was going to happen at our house, if my father would go off into a rage, if my mother would flip out and go on a crying or drinking binge, if my father would get into a fight with my brother Robert, or if the police would show up. Worse, I never knew what my father would say to my girl-friends. He always found a way to interject himself in their visits. Some of my friends seemed to elicit more attention than others.

"Hello Nicole," my father said rounding the corner from the living room. "You're looking good." He stood too close to her and stared at her breasts. "How are the boys treating you?"

"Fine," she said, turning red in her cheeks.

"I'm going to see your mom a bit later. I'll have to remind her to keep your chastity belt on tight. Real tight. What are you girls going to do tonight?"

"We're waiting for Susan and Beth to come over," I said, trying to usher Nicole out of the room.

"Well, don't get into any trouble while you're here," he said to Nicole as he hugged her too close. "What size are you now. Let me guess, 34C?"

"Dad, gross." I wanted to die. Scream. Disappear. But I also didn't want to draw attention to his disgusting habits.

"Gorgeous as ever. Your old lady did good. Good to see you, Nicole."

"Good to see you too, Mr. Close," she said, giggling.

"Gross," I said to Nicole, cringing inside.

"He's harmless."

I heard Beth and Susan's footsteps as they tromped up the steps to the porch.

"Sorry, we're late," Beth said.

"Pino's?" I asked.

"I thought we were hanging out here," Susan said.

"I second Pino's," Nicole said.

"Pino's it is."

I grabbed my coat. "Let me just go tell my Dad where we're going." In the kitchen, without looking at him, I announced, "We're going to Pino's."

"Don't the girls want to have dinner here? We have plenty of food," he said.

"Nope. We're going to Pino's."

"Alright, but come home right after. No gallivanting around. Are the girls staying over?"

"I don't know," I said, lying. "We'll figure it out later." I turned, walked back to the front door where the girls were waiting. "Let's go," I said. "Before he changes his mind."

As we walked down to the trolley, I pulled a pack of Larks from my handbag, lit one up and took a deep, hard drag. It was risky to smoke in public, but I didn't care. "God, why does he have to do that?" I thought. "Why can't he just ask what other parents ask and let everyone alone. I hate him for ruining my night. What else will go wrong tonight?"

"Ellen, helloo, El-len?" Nicole said. "I don't mean to interrupt the deep conversation you're having with yourself, but there's Karen. Do you want to invite her?"

"Sure."

"You okay?"

"Yeah, fine."

I dreaded the rest of the night, wanted to run away. Why couldn't I just let it go like Nicole seemed to? Had she let it go, or would she wait until I wasn't there and tell Susan and Beth what my father said? I wished I could be at the Cape with Danny and his friends where I didn't have to worry about being humiliated this way.

We stood on the median at Cleveland Circle, trying to cross the street. I was smoking. I noticed my father's mustard Mercedes. He saw me and braked so hard there was a loud screech. Everyone turned to stare.

He jumped out of the car, screaming, "You look like a hooker, a goddamn hooker. No daughter of mine is going to look like a hooker." He hit me across the face, grabbed me by the arm and shoved me in the backseat. Susan looked panicked. He slammed my door shut, jumped in the driver's seat and sped off, squealing the tires. He kept hitting me with his right hand. "You're nothing but a worthless piece of shit, and you'll never amount to anything," he screamed as he slapped my head and shoulders. This was a familiar refrain. He'd scream this at me at least once or twice a week, or more, often for no reason.

When we pulled up to the house, I was too afraid to move.

"So help me God, you get in that house now, or I will kill you."

I wanted to wait until he walked in the house to get out of the car, but he didn't budge. I got out and made my way up the peeling wooden front steps.

He followed saying, "You're shit," as he kicked my upper thighs and butt again and again. I managed to stumble up the stairs. "Do you like how that feels?" he screamed. "You want to act like a whore, that's how you'll get treated."

Once in the door, he told me to go to my room.

"I will be up there in a minute to take care of this," he said in such a calm, matter-of-fact voice, I got chills and began sweating and shaking. He did not sound like my father, not even the rageful father.

I had no choice but to go to my room and wait for my beating. I blacked out from this point forward. I can't remember anything except a vivid memory that comes up in therapy and in some of my nightmares. My father's brown leather shoe was kicking me again and again in the rib cage as I lay on my back on my bedroom floor. "You're nothing but a worthless piece of shit," he screamed. I couldn't catch my breath. The air didn't feel like it was getting to my lungs.

"Stop," I cried. He only kicked me harder.

The next thing I remember is that I was lying on my bed rolled up into a fetal position on my left side.

Years later, my mother told me that she was petrified he was going to beat me to death. His rage was beyond her control, but she was too scared to call the police or anyone else.

She said she screamed at him until he stopped. I was never taken to a hospital or to see a doctor. My mother came to my room sometime later to try and comfort me, and I told her to leave me alone.

When I awoke the next morning, I was black and blue everywhere and had welts on my legs and stomach. My left eye was swollen. My body ached down to my bones. I could barely move without wincing. I stayed in bed most of that day.

Nothing more was ever said. We were all expected to go on with our lives as if nothing had happened.

Kitchen Cupboards

"Oh God, no!" I screamed. My mother was splayed flat on her back on the den floor. I walked towards her body. I was 14 or 15; I could never remember. My life from that time was foggy. "Mom! Mom!" She did not move.

As if in a dream, I watched myself take action, grabbing the phone on the end table, dialing 911. A woman answered. In a trembling voice, I said, "I think my mother's dead."

The woman stayed calm. "Okay, now we are going to work together on this alright?" she said in a motherly tone. "Where exactly is your mother right now?"

"She's lying on the floor in front of me, but she's not moving. She looks dead."

"And what's your name?"

"Ellen."

"Okay, is there anything else around your mother?"

"An ashtray."

"Is there anything sharp, like broken glass?"

"No. But the whole room smells like alcohol."

"Can you kneel down and feel or hear if she's breathing?"

I knelt down scared to death to find out if she was breathing. "Yes, she's breathing. But why doesn't she move or wake up?"

"We're going to try and figure that out. Does your mother have a drinking problem?"

"Sometimes, sort of. Only once in a while when she's not feeling good."

"Do you know if she's on any kind of medication?"

"Yes, she takes pills for her mental illness."

"Do you know where she keeps her pills?"

"Yes, in the bathroom."

"Okay, I want you to go into the bathroom and see if you can find the pill bottles for me."

"Okay, but is it okay to leave her alone?"

"She'll be okay, honey. I'll be right here."

I put the phone down and walked into the bathroom. A torn facial towel hung off the edge of the sink, two large orange prescription pill bottles and a smaller bottle and caps were strewn over the tiny corner sink. Two large bottles of vodka and rum sat on the back of the toilet, both more than half empty. The bathroom reeked of alcohol, burnt cigarettes and rubbing alcohol.

I ran back to the phone. "Oh, no, there's a mess everywhere. Her bottles are empty. There's two big bottles of booze and lots of cigarettes burned to their bottom."

"Okay. Do you have the pill bottles, Ellen?"

"Yes."

"Good. I want you to read to me exactly what it says on the bottles." They were drugs like Lithium and some kind of sleeping pills. I gave her all the information I could find.

"Excellent. I want you to go and get a kettle and make some hot water. Can you do that?"

"Yes." I was afraid to put the phone down. "You sure you'll still be here?"

"I'll be right here. I won't hang up. I'm sending help. They're on their way right now. Is there a number where your father can be reached?"

"No, he's on the Cape doing business."

"Okay, is there another relative we could call, or a friend of the family?"

Dr. Sabrinsky came to my mind. She was a psychiatrist and my best friend's mother who adored me. I was afraid to tell the woman her name. I knew my father would kill me for involving anyone else. "Dr. Sabrinsky," I said. She asked for the number. I knew it by heart and gave it to her.

"Okay, is there any coffee in the house?"

"Yes, my mother drinks coffee."

"We are going to make some coffee for your Mom, okay?"

"Okay." In the kitchen, I could hear the sirens coming down the road. I was surprisingly calm.

Suddenly firemen swarmed the house. One asked me to show him the bathroom. As we stood next to the sink, I began to shake uncontrollably, and bent over the toilet and threw up. With the fireman standing there, I felt even more scared. His presence made the moment more real. I couldn't deny that my mother was ill. I couldn't deny that she had tried to take her own life.

I could hear another fireman talking with a woman. It was Dr. Sabrinsky. Then there was a strange silence. I ran into the den and found them sitting my mother up, flashing light into her eyes and calling her name. Dr. Sabrinsky had me go and get a cup of the coffee. When I came back, she was giving my mother a shot.

"I don't need your help," my mother slurred. "I'm fine. I'm good. Leave me be."

"Jackie, you need to go to the hospital," Dr. Sabrinsky said.

"I don't need help. Just leave me alone."

"We can't leave you like this."

"No." My mother started crying. "I won't go anyplace. I'm home. I'm fine. I just want to sleep. Just let me sleep.

The doctor explained that my mom really needed to go to the hospital. She would have to commit her unless my mother went willingly. I agreed, but was scared to death my father would kill me for calling 911, for getting Dr. Sabrinsky involved and for letting people know what was going on. I heard his voice: "Nothing ever goes on here. Do you hear me? Nothing ever goes on here."

"Jackie, we need to take you to the hospital," Dr. Sabrinsky said.

"No," my mother screamed. "They will hurt me. Ellen, don't let them hurt me."

Two medics hoisted my mother onto a stretcher. She flailed her arms, and they strapped her down.

"Don't let then hurt me, Ellen."

As they carried her out, she said in a mean drunken voice, "I will get you for this. You'll see."

She was hospitalized in a private mental institution. I prayed they'd treat her better than the one I had remembered. I was not permitted to visit her. All the other kids went to visit each week. My father told me she felt that I had been through enough. I saw it differently. It was her way of getting even with me for committing her.

On a Wednesday evening at dinner, one month after they took my mother away on a stretcher, my father announced that she'd be coming home that Saturday.

"Ellen, your mom's going to need your help."

"Okay."

"She's still a little fuzzy, but she's getting stronger every day."

"Fuzzy like what?" I flashed to the woman in the station wagon at the mental institution so many years ago. I prayed he didn't mean fuzzy and strange like *that*.

"Just a little slower."

"Dad…"

"Ellen, be nice to her."

"Okay, okay."

For the next two days, I scrubbed the house clean and did all the laundry. At night, alone in my room, I spent hours gazing at the pictures of my mother I had collected over the years. There was one of her in short shorts on visiting day at Camp Naticook where my fellow campers mistook her for being my older sister, a black and white wedding photo in which she looked like one of the darling starlets of the 50's, the baby picture that I first thought was me, a picture of her in a smashing brown bell bottom one piece with a fur trimmed collar that I'd always wanted, one of me wrapped up in a baby blanket in her arms, and one of her and my dad on a Cape Cod beach smiling. While I fantasized about how much fun it would be to have her home, my stomach did full-out gymnastics.

The day she came home, winter was just giving way in New England. It was a windy, brisk day. As I ran around the house cleaning off the kitchen counters and making sure everything was in its right place, I knew it wouldn't matter to my mother. She didn't care about a clean house. Still, I couldn't stop myself.

When Dad arrived with her, I could hear all the other kids' excitement coming from the living room.

"Ellen, Mom's home."

I stayed in the kitchen wiping the last counter. I tried to breathe normally, but couldn't because of a lump in my throat. Finally, I went into the living room in time to watch her walk up our old wooden stairs. She hung onto the wooden banister as if she would fall without it. My heart sank. I ran back into the kitchen and wiped the kitchen counters again. I was afraid to see her. This her. I was afraid of what she was going to say to me or not say to me. Feeling awkward and shy, I would have run away if I could have. My father's voice stuck in my head, "Ellen, be nice to her." The air felt like it got stuck in my throat, like it was too thick to make its way to my lungs. What if she never talked to me again? What if she spat at me? What if?

I could hear her footsteps close to the kitchen entrance, and hugged the kitchen counter. She stood staring at me with a haunting blank stare. Was I supposed to give her a hug? Or stand there and let her come to me? Was I supposed to act like nothing had ever happened and just say, "Hi Mom"?

"Hello, Ellen," she said in that distant way I remembered from years ago. My body felt ice cold. "You did a nice job cleaning the house."

Her words felt fake, forced, flat and phony as if she were being told what to say and repeating meaningless words. Every ounce of my being wanted to scream at her, "What is wrong with you? Why did you try and kill yourself? Why can't you just be my mother?" I knew everyone had already denied it. My father was standing too close behind her watching me. His voice was in my head again, "Nothing ever goes on here. Do you hear me?"

"It's nice to see you," I managed to get out of my cotton dry mouth.

She didn't seem to hear me. She looked at the cabinets in a weird way as if she were lost. She jerked back and forth and started weeping.

"Where are the drinking cups? I don't see any drinking glasses."

I grabbed a drinking glass from the cabinet to her right. "They're here, Mom. They're right here."

"Aren't they supposed to be here?" She pointed to the cabinet to the left.

"Mom, they're here, remember." I opened the cabinet where they'd always been and showed her an assortment of glasses.

"Oh, right," she said, calming down.

One by one, I took her through each of the cabinets while my father looked on. She seemed puzzled as she looked through each cabinet. Nothing had changed, except her.

"Thank you," she said. "I'll remember now."

"Remember," I wanted to scream. "How could you have forgotten? You have lived here with the same cabinets for three whole years. How could you have forgotten?" Instead, I gave her my best attempt at a smile.

"It's good to be home." She looked at my father and the rest of the kitchen.

The word home pierced through my skin as if I had been shot with a bullet. "I'd give anything, Mom, for you to be home," I said silently in my head.

Dad took her upstairs to their bedroom so she could rest. He insisted that I help him prepare dinner. We made pork chops, apple sauce and broccoli with cheddar cheese sauce and fried onion rings. We all did our best to act as if we were one happy family just having another Saturday night dinner. My mother sat quietly taking small bites of food as if she were a well-behaved child. As we were finishing, she blurted out, in that far away voice, "Ellen, I want to talk with you in private."

We went to their bedroom. They sat on the end of their bed, and I sat in a chair opposite. In a flat tone, she said, "The doctors and I have agreed that I need to tell you how I feel about you."

I picked some lint off of my wool socks.

"I don't love you," she said.

A sharp, stabbing pain shot though my chest. Barely breathing, I nodded, stood up, walked out and ran up the stairs to my bedroom. I fell onto my bed, buried my head in the pillow and shrieked tears of pain.

Leaving Home

"For God's sake, Ellen, why the fuck did you just pile everything up in the hallway?"

I looked over at Michael, and we rolled our eyes. I knew better than to answer. It wasn't a real question. I just wanted to get to college.

Ever since my father had shown me the door as my only other option to college, we hadn't been getting along. I had withdrawn from him and his craziness and barely spoke in full sentences. I was surprised when he announced that he and my mother would drive me to school and help me move in. We were supposed to have left at "10 a.m. sharp". I should have known better. My father lived on his own timetable. One business call led to another. By 2, he was finally ready.

I picked up a pile and began to carry it out to the car.

"Don't put that in first," he yelled from the front porch. "I'll give Michael what goes in first."

I put my pile down on the curb and went back into the house to get another load. "I'll pile it up, and you just tell me where to put it." I thought, "Instead of putting so much effort into packing the damn car, what would have really helped was having a home I wasn't being thrown out of, assistance figuring out which schools to apply to, and help preparing for the SATs."

After taking the SATs, I overheard kids talking about how the prep class had really helped. I never knew a prep class was an option. My life had moved into this strange mix of hyper speed locomotion and numb overload. I couldn't remember how I figured out which schools to apply to. Somehow, I was accepted to Syracuse University.

By the time we finished, it was past 3. Michael and I crawled into the back seat between loads of hefty bags filled with my clothes, towels and blankets. My mother took her customary place in the front passenger seat next to my father. My father had asked Michael to come so he could practice his driving skills and help with the drive home.

I took a deep breath and prayed my father's mood would lighten. We had a five-hour drive from Brookline to Syracuse. I wasn't moving into the dorm until the following day, but I had hoped that we could get there early and have a celebratory dinner before we went back to the hotel for the night. Since we'd started so late, that wasn't going to happen. We'd eat at a truck stop. As long as my father's mood didn't worsen, I decided it'd be okay.

We pulled into the university a little after 10 and drove directly to the dorm. Why wasn't he going to the hotel? I didn't dare ask. His mood wasn't good. In front of the dorm, he said, "Ellie, go in and see if you can move in."

Thrown off guard, I said, "Dad, I'm not supposed to move in until tomorrow. Can't we just go to the hotel and go to sleep?"

"It's late, and we might as well just drive home tonight."

My mind scrambled for a way to convince him to go to the hotel.

"I'm sure it'll be fine. Just go and see. It's late. We have a long drive home. I'm sure they'll be fine."

I got out of the car. Against the cool night air, my face and ears were burning. As I walked into the dorm, I didn't know if anyone would be there. Part of me prayed someone would be there and another part of me prayed no one would. I took the elevator to the second floor and as it opened, a woman seemed to be waiting for me.

"Hi, I'm Jennifer. I'm the RA. Can I help you?"

"Hi, I'm Ellen Close. I'm supposed to move in tomorrow."

"Yes, room 246. Welcome."

I couldn't believe she knew my room number off the top of her head. Her razor sharp, almost military precision impressed me but also made me want to laugh.

"Do you want to see your room?"

"Well, actually, I want to know if it'd be possible if I could move my stuff in. My father isn't feeling well, and they just want to drive back home tonight."

"Oh, I'm sorry. Well, I don't see why not. Another one of your floor mates had to move in today as well. Do you need help?"

"No thanks. My brother can help me. Thanks so much."

Riding down the elevator, I wanted to cry but knew I had to keep it together. This day should have gone so differently. After the celebratory dinner, we would've spent the day unpacking before my parents left with tears in their eyes and tight hugs goodbye. Instead, I was forced to lie to cover for my father's craziness and would be left alone in this cold empty building. It dawned on me that my father had planned this all along. That was why he asked Michael to come. Had he even made a reservation at a hotel? I wanted to scream, cry and kick something, anything, but I knew better. My father would make an even bigger scene.

I opened the car door. "It's fine. I can move in."

"You see, what did I tell you, Ellie? Get in, and I'll drive you closer to the front."

My mother sat quietly. Why didn't she say something? I wanted her to say, "Lennie, this is not right. This is no way to celebrate our daughter starting college. Come on, let's go back to the hotel and begin again tomorrow."

Michael and I unpacked the car in record time. As we took the elevator down after the last load, my stomach knotted up and a lump formed in my throat. My father was standing by the car.

"Ellie, we gotta go. It's late and we have a long drive home." He reached out and gave me a huge hug. I wanted to throw up, scream and cry.

I walked around to the passenger side of the car. "I'll miss you, Mom." I gave her a hug.

"I'll miss you too, honey. Call us tomorrow."

I stood alone on the curb under the dark night sky and stared as they pulled away in the empty car. Once they were out of sight, I felt exhausted, shaky and vacant.

I decided to take pre-med courses. I wasn't sure where my inspiration came from. My father had always wanted me to become a wife first, and a corporate vice president, second. He was certain that I had a knack for business. But in our extended family, being a doctor was highly respected. He spoke highly of our great Uncle Morrie, a family doctor who was beloved by both the community and more importantly, by my grandmother, the same grandmother who had shown no love for my father.

My decision unraveled during my first physics class. I was one of three women. At every turn, the professor tried to prove that women were not cut out for the sciences. During an experiment with a male classmate, he started laughing at the way I was explaining something.

"Miss Close," he said, "You really think you are cut out for this? Your explanation hardly holds water. Mark, please explain to Miss Close why her thinking is completely erroneous."

After class, I went to the Dean's office and complained. The Dean's assistant whispered, "You won't have much luck with this. Why don't you just drop the class and take it next semester. It'll be taught by a different professor."

Clearly, the department was aware of his antics and chose to do nothing. I thanked her and marched to the registrar's office and dropped the class.

I did my best to focus on school, but I often found myself cramming the night before, a habit I had refined in high school. My latest test result, with its prominent red C, proved I couldn't get away with it in college. Not wanting anyone to see the test, I kept folding it until it looked like a small origami box. The message was clear. If I was planning on doing well at Syracuse, cramming wasn't going to cut it.

My roommate was out at her cafeteria job that afternoon. I found it difficult to focus around other people, and never understood the concept of group study. The snow had just started coming down hard. My room felt cozy, warm and quiet. I sat back on my baby blue bed bolster, pulled out all my syllabi, looked at all of my classes and made a list of assignment deadlines. Why hadn't I done this earlier? Even though overwhelmed by all the work ahead of me, I was calmed by attending to it. I grabbed the largest hardback off the floor, my psychology text. It was an easy read, and I could whip through it.

"Ellen, phone," John yelled down the dormitory hall.

I grabbed my bag and ran down the hall. "Hello?"

"I'm gonna fucking throw her out on the street if she doesn't straighten up. You better do something with her, Ellen, or I swear to God, I will put her out on the street. Do you hear me?" My father screamed like a lunatic on the other end of the line.

"Dad, Dad," I said, twirling the telephone cord around my index finger.

He kept screaming, loud and garbled, and I couldn't make sense of what he was saying. I held the phone away from my ear and prayed he'd calm down.

He said more clearly, "If you don't want your mother on the street, then I suggest you talk some sense into her. Do you hear me?"

Wendy, one of the prettiest girls on our floor, walked by in her bopping stride, with her perennial broad smile. "Ta, ta, lovey," she said, tapping my head. I smiled at her, pretending everything was just great.

"Dad, can I speak to Mom?" I kept my voice low so Wendy and the others couldn't hear.

"You've got five minutes."

I looked out from the open phone cubby and prayed no one was waiting to use the phone.

"Hello," my mother said in a weak voice.

I could still hear my father's breath on the phone. "Dad, let me talk to Mom alone, okay?" I heard a click, then another. He was still on the line. "Dad, I need to talk to Mom alone." The phone clicked just once. "Mom, what's going on?"

"You know your father. Does it have to be anything?" She dragged hard on her Salem.

"Mom, what are you going to do?" I fumbled through my bag for a cigarette. I cupped the phone. "Mom, I can't do this from here."

"Ellen, don't worry. You know your father is just full of threats. Tomorrow will be different. I'll be okay. I'll call you to-morrow. Don't worry."

"Mom…"

"Ellen, I gotta go."

The line clicked, and there was a dial tone. I stood looking at the phone, wanting run to the airport and get on the next

plane home. I didn't have money for a flight. I didn't know
what to do.

I managed to walk to my room, and collapse on the bed.
Crying so hard, I bruised one of my ribs. I spotted myself in
the mirror and gasped. The eyes looking back at me were those
of my depressed mother. Was this really my face? "Dear God,"
I prayed, "please do not let me become like her. Please, I beg
of you." As I scrubbed my face extra hard, the phone down the
hall rang. One ring, two, three. Someone picked it up on the
fourth ring. I clutched at my stomach. "Dear God, please don't
let it be him. Please."

"Ellen...Close, phone's for you." John yelled as he banged
on the door. I didn't want to answer it, but if it was him and
he was throwing her out, I had to know.

I grabbed the dangling phone. "Hello?"

"Ellen, it's Mom. Dad went out to run an errand."

I burst into tears. "Mom, you okay? What happened?"

"The same thing that always happens. He didn't like the
meatloaf."

"Mom, I want to come home. I hate being this far away. I
can't study anyway."

"Ellen, I'm fine. You need to stay in school. Just worry
about you, okay?" she said. "Dad's going to be home soon, I
gotta go."

"You promise you'll call me if anything else happens."

"I promise. Don't worry. I'm fine," she said with an odd
lilt in her voice.

As I got off the phone, I started thinking about her voice.
It wasn't steady. Had she been drinking? One part of me didn't
want to know, couldn't know. Thanksgiving wasn't that far
away. What could happen in just a few short months?

I made the mistake of going to my room and lying down
on my bed. As soon as my head hit the pillow, my mind swirled
in vivid technicolor of my mother's past faces, battered,

bruised, terrified and depressed. I shot straight up, needing something to occupy my mind. Studying would certainly be the smart thing to do, but I wasn't in any mood. Laundry didn't take too much brain power. I gathered my pile in the closet and went to the basement. Listening to the clothes chugging through their cycles, I was able to calm down. The drone of the washers and dryers drowned out the bad mother faces. I loved the smell of the fresh detergent.

The exhaustion of worry overtook my body. I slumped lower into the red plastic chair, my eyes getting heavy. I wished I was a baby wrapped in a soft white blanket held by a yummy mummy. My head jerked. Without realizing it, I'd dozed off. The thump, thump, thump of the washing machine woke me. I heard voices coming down the hall.

Wendy walked into the laundry room with her gal pal Lorna. "Hello, beautiful. My friend Jake thinks you're real cute. He'd love to set you up with his friend David. Sweet, sweet David from Jersey. What do you say? Are you game?"

I wondered if she ever thought about anything other than getting her M.R.S. degree. I smiled. "I'll think about it."

"Come on. You'll like him. He's cute."

If you knew what my day had been like you'd know that thinking about some sweet, sweet David was the last fucking thing that I'd be doing. "Sure," I said, "make a date." I grabbed my clothes out of the washer and threw them in the dryer.

"Wait," squealed Wendy, "you're putting all that stuff into one dryer?"

"Yeah…"

"There's too much. They won't dry nicely."

"You're serious?"

"Seriously," she said, giggling. "Isn't that right, Lorna?"

"Whatever, Miss Queen," Lorna shrugged.

I wanted to put Wendy into the dryer. I wanted to scream at her to get real about life. "Thanks, but my clothes seem to get done just fine."

"Alright but you'll see. Just thought I'd give you a tip," she said in her higher, too cheery voice.

I stared at her in disbelief. Had she ever had a day like mine? Had she ever had to worry about her mother committing suicide or her father killing her mother? I must have stared too long.

"Sorry," said Wendy, "I just thought I'd share what my Mom taught me."

"Thanks, I'll keep it in mind."

"Anyway, we're on for a foursome?"

"Sure." I could feel my face burning with a mixture of anger and sadness.

"You okay?" Wendy asked, sorting her laundry into piles.

I paused. I was desperate to tell someone what was going on, but looking at Wendy sorting her laundry as though that were the most important thing in life, I knew she could never deal with my life. "I'm fine, just a little tired."

"Sleep always helps me."

"Yeah, sleep would be good." I wished I could actually sleep.

"I'll call and make a plan with the guys for next week. Okay?"

"A plan will be good."

"Ta, ta," she said in her light airy voice. "Latah."

As soon as I heard the door bang behind Wendy and Lorna, I draped myself over the dryer like a wet dishcloth. Large soupy tears fell onto the machine.

"Dear God, please help me," I whispered. "Why can't I just have a normal life with normal parents you can depend on? Are you really there, God? I need you to be there. Promise me you're there." I pulled a pack of cigarettes from my laundry bag, slumped in the chair, threw my legs up on the dryer, yanked a Marlboro out of the red and white box, lit it and took a deep, hard drag. "Fuck, I just wish I could be like everybody else. If you're so mighty, why can't you just let me wake up and have a normal life? Is that really too much to ask? Ask and ye shall receive, right? That's what it says. Well, I'm asking. Let me just wake up and be normal." I took one last drag. "I'll even take just one day. Just one normal day."

The phone calls and my father's threats continued. I developed a strange tightness in my chest that I chose to ignore. Worry about my mom and siblings became constant companions. Even though I had made some good friends, I felt singular. I didn't tell anyone about my family. No one at school would understand. I barely did. Right before Thanksgiving, I caved under the mounting pressure and decided to leave school. I would go home and tell my parents over the Thanksgiving break.

I arrived at my parents' house on the Tuesday before Thanksgiving Day for the first time since I'd left for college. Everything felt the same except for me. I was utterly exhausted. Even the large sweater that I'd begun wearing to hide my too-tight jeans seemed limp with fatigue. I couldn't wait to sleep in my own bed, for our Thanksgiving Day feast and even the background noise of the football games. Just the thought of the turkey roasting all day with stuffing dripping with butter made me feel warm and fuzzy.

The first full day home felt amazing. My father was happy and celebratory. My parents seemed at ease and loving with one another. All my anxiety from the semester evaporated. It was good to be home. Given everyone's mood, I thought it was a great time to tell them my news. Early that evening after dinner, my father was sitting doing some paperwork at his desk.

"Dad, can we talk for a minute?"

"What's up?" he asked, not looking up.

"Well," I said, taking a deep breath, "I've decided that I'm not going to go back to school. I think it would be better for me to be here at home."

"Ellen," he said, raising his eyes above his glasses, "I thought I made myself perfectly clear. You leave school, you leave here. You're on your own. Period. Do you hear me?" He turned back to his work.

"I'm not going back," I yelled at him.

"Fine, you want to leave, then leave. No daughter of mine is a quitter."

"I'm not a quitter," I yelled back at him. "It's my choice."

"And it's my choice who lives here. You want to quit then go pack your fucking bags, and get the hell out of here."

I ran up the stairs to my bedroom, screaming, "I hate you, I really do. You know that. I hate you." I slammed my door and smashed my body on my bed. Didn't he get that all of his stupid phone calls were too much stress on me? At least if I was home, I could see what was going on. I could try and keep him from going crazy on my mother, and I wouldn't be constantly worrying about everyone here.

There was no safe place for me. I wanted to jump out of my skin. Was this what it felt like when my mother started to go crazy? I got up and looked at myself in the mirror. Black under-eye circles accentuated by sallow skin made it obvious that I wasn't thriving. My eyes reminded me of her eyes right before she went into a downward spiral that would land her in the hospital.

I returned to school feeling more isolated and alone. There was no going back home. I'd be a welcomed visitor for school breaks, but otherwise I was on my own. Fortunately, within the first week of the new semester, I met Margaret and Dr. Hall.

Margaret was a counselor at Syracuse. I met her by chance while looking for a substitute class. At that time, I would never have had the courage or desire to look for help from anyone. My father thought if you asked for help you were crazy.

Margaret mostly guided people into suitable majors.

Under the auspices of trying to figure out my major, I began meeting with her weekly. In a short span of time, I told her about my desire to leave school and move back home, and my father's refusal. I was not quite sure how I explained my family, but I was certain it was in code. Back then, I held to the notion that we were a nice Jewish family. Margaret became my staunchest ally to stay in school. She was someone with whom I could shed tears without too many questions. In her, I came to feel a great comfort.

Dr. Hall, a Comparative Religion professor, was a broad man of about 6'1" with astute grey blue eyes. He had a rare talent for making each one of his students feel special. I could tell his heart was filled with a deep compassion for the world's suffering, especially for those who had in any way been harmed by what he referred to as "religious righteousness, condemnation, pious zealousness and racism." He would not suffer any of this nonsense. "In this classroom, we will honor and respect one another so that we may enter into true dialogue even and especially when our religious differences and ideas vary or are at odds with one another. By doing so, each one of you will teach the world that true compassion, respect, understanding and religious freedom is indeed possible." My heart and soul felt at home just sitting in his class.

He had an open door policy and was always available during his office hours and welcomed conversations on any topic. I often stopped in towards the end of his office hours hoping to have a private conversation. We began a conversation about God and life that semester that carried on through my junior year at Syracuse. In Dr. Hall, I had found a place to rest.

During junior midterms, my mom was on my mind constantly. I hadn't heard from my parents in weeks. It was too quiet. One Friday when I could afford a break from my studies, I called home.

My father answered. "Hey Ellie, how's school going?" he

asked in an upbeat tone.

"Fine. Can I talk with Mom?"

"She's not here."

"What do you mean she's not there?"

"I threw her out."

"What? When?"

"Ellen, it's over."

"Dad, you can't just tell me you threw her out of the house and think that I'm gonna be fine. Where is she?"

"I have no idea."

"When did this happen?"

"Last night."

My mind went into hyper speed. I imagined my mother wandering the streets without a coat. Without shoes. Naked. Drunk. Lying in a gutter. Not knowing her own name.

"Dad, is Robert there? Let me talk with Robert."

"He's out."

"Dad, where is she?"

"Ellen, just face it, she's gone."

"You can't just do this. What is wrong with you?"

"This is between your mother and me. I don't have to answer to you or anybody else." I heard a click, then a dial tone.

I stared at the phone. My mind raced. What should I do? I needed to find someone to talk to, but didn't know to whom to turn. My rabbi's face flashed in my brain. I'd seen a flyer for a synagogue on the bulletin board in Meany Hall and remembered the address. I went to my room, grabbed my coat and bag and drove in the pouring rain to the temple.

Drenched from running from the car, I should have known by the way only men were sitting on the main floor that I had entered an Orthodox temple. I was blinded by the storm of my emotions. I took a seat on the main floor, and the men's eyes turned towards me. I thought, "No I am not moving. Women have the right to sit wherever they want to sit and you can't make me move." Whispers echoed through the temple.

An older man with a long white beard approached and asked in a hushed tone, "Are you Jewish, my friend?"

"Yes."

"There are plenty of seats upstairs with the other women."

"Thank you, but I am happy with my seat."

"I'm sorry, I don't think you understand. You belong upstairs with the other women, in the women's area. Only men sit here."

"I'm sorry, I'd like to sit here and pray. I'm not interested in sitting with the women and gossiping."

"Women don't sit here," he reiterated. "You will either need to move upstairs with the other women or leave."

"And you say you are God's people? How do you know God doesn't want women to sit here?" I spoke loud enough for everyone, including the women sitting upstairs, to hear me.

"I'm sorry. You will need to leave unless you sit up there in the women's section."

I stood up. "I will be happy to leave," I yelled louder. "Women aren't second class citizens as you believe them to be. And I will not be treated like I am nothing but cattle. I will not be treated as if I don't count." My ears burned with indignation. My heart felt like it was being stabbed. I found it hard to breathe.

I ran and sat in my oversized black Buick and wept. "What is wrong with these people? God, is this what you want? Who the fuck cares where you sit? Is that what's really important?"

"That's it." I wiped my eyes and blew my nose. "I am done with this stupid religion and their stupid, asinine ways. I am done. I will never step foot in a temple again. I will never believe in a religion that makes women second class citizens."

As I drove, I recounted the ways the Jewish religion made women act stupid. Women were more than just pretty objects traipsing around in the latest fashions and diamond earrings.

No matter how beautiful, I knew clothes didn't define a person's heart or true character. How could it be that women didn't count enough to make up a minion? If we are all God's children, how come only men count to make up a minion? I sobbed and argued with the men back at the temple. "What makes you think only you know what God thinks?" I hadn't given up God, but I was finished with organized religion.

Something inside me popped. My anger abated. As a cold silence permeated me, I felt utterly alone. Despair seeped through my veins. I was being dragged in a downward spiral by a tumultuous current. I fought hard to hold onto my fight, the only way I knew to survive, but even that was slipping away.

I was losing everything I had always known as home.

The Call

My mother came back a few days after she left. I didn't know if my father went after her. I wanted to believe he did, that somewhere deep inside he knew he was wrong. She called when she returned. She'd gone to Betty Harvey's house. Betty was one of her only true friends. She was as big as my father.

During my remaining years at Syracuse, I made myself numb to my parents' still-regular phone calls. They seemed to have an unnatural ability to recover from their lethal fights and go back to pretending everything was fine. I didn't possess that knack. As dating and school took priority, I became less accessible.

Senior year, I met a law student named Jeffrey. I had the honor of being one of the four undergrads chosen to compete side-by-side with the law students in Moot Court, an extracurricular activity where participants took part in simulated court proceedings. Jeff was in his last year of law school. He was everything my father had dreamed a husband for me should be, Jewish, smart, non-threatening and from a well-to-do family. He was the man that "could keep me in the style to which

I had become accustomed to". We married the December after I graduated from Syracuse on my parents' anniversary. My father chose the date.

Jeffrey and I moved to New York City into an apartment on 45th across the street from the UN. It was a small one bedroom with paper-thin walls on the 26th floor. The open sky view gave it the illusion of space.

"Leave me alone," I screamed at Jeffrey in the middle of the living room.

"There you go again," he said folding his arms. "You're so angry. Ellen."

"Yup, that's right. It's always about my anger. Just because you never raise your voice, you think you're perfect."

Jeffrey stood as still as a statue.

I picked up the lamp sitting on the coffee table and threw it towards the floor in his direction. "There. You're right. You're absolutely right. I'm just one angry bitch."

"You see," he said in the soft monotone voice. "You'll never change. No matter what you say, you see, you never keep your word. You're just like your father."

I went into the bedroom and began ripping the bed apart. "You want to see angry. Fine, you'll see angry," I screamed at the top of my lungs, enjoying myself. I knew I was out of control, but I was also reveling in getting this out once and for all. Across the bedroom I saw a photo album of one of our vacations. I picked it up and threw it at the wall in the other room. "Who needs these fucking memories?" I picked the album up, ripped the first page out and pulled a photo from behind its plastic covering. We were smiling on a white sandy beach in Bermuda. "Ha, total bullshit," I screamed as I shredded it, knowing damn well it would crush his heart.

Jeff didn't move. He wouldn't react. His lack of reaction made me feel crazy.

"You're right, Jeffrey," I screamed. "You're absolutely right. Does that feel good? Is that what you want? To be right. Good, now you're goddamn R-I-G-H-T. Right, right, right."

A picture flashed in my mind's eye of my father saying these exact words. It horrified me, but I didn't want to stop; I couldn't stop. It felt too good. I began pounding the bed. "I hate you. I fucking hate you. Do you hear me? I hate you."

The buzzer rang. Our eyes met. In that moment, we were once again on the same team. In unison, we scrunched our faces and shoulders up towards our ears. We knew it was yet another complaint from a neighbor. I managed to take a breath, walk over to the intercom and press the button.

"Hello," I said breathless.

"Mrs. Newhouse? It's Tony. Another neighbor has called complaining. Please, can you keep your voices down? It's late."

I could feel my face burning with shame. This was not the cheery Mrs. Newhouse Tony knew. It wasn't the person I wanted anyone to know, including myself.

Jeff and I fought often and hard. It was a tumultuous relationship. Neither one of us had learned healthy skills to build a strong foundation. Jeffrey's parents were also enmeshed in a dysfunctional relationship. We'd fight over just about anything. It wasn't the content of our arguments that mattered.

What I didn't know then was that we were both fighting our parents through our relationship. I was fighting for control, my right to exist, power and to feel loved. Jeffrey was railing against his mother and her need to dominate. I felt controlled by Jeffrey and was obsessed with having control over myself where my mother did not. Determined not to lose the battle against my father vis-a-vis Jeffrey, I fought hard.

Even though I loved Jeffrey, I often felt overwhelmed, out of control and suffocated. I hated our fights, was ashamed by how I screamed, and made countless futile promises to myself to never fight with him again. It was as if the person who was fighting wasn't me. I had no control over her hurt, grief, anger or rage and couldn't even break those feelings down. They were bundled into a blur of tears and rage. I hated to admit to myself that we weren't doing any better than my parents. And I couldn't believe how mean I could be to him. After all I had experienced with my dad and witnessed between my mom and dad, I was horrified to observe myself carrying out the exact same tactical maneuvers of my father. When I calmed down, I shivered at the similarities. I knew better, but I couldn't seem to do better in the moment. For years I had promised myself I would never act like my father or my mother. And yet, I had become a high-wired grenade.

Later, I'd come to understand that almost none of it had to do with Jeffrey and most everything to do with my unresolved issues with both my parents. He was not only a good trigger; he was the perfect trigger. It would take years of therapy and soul searching to begin to understand the complexity of our relationship and my emotions.

The phone rang at 5 a.m. one hot summer morning. Out of my sleep, my hand picked up the receiver. "Hello?"

"Ellen, it's Maida." Before I had fully opened my eyes, I heard my friend Maida bawling. I could barely understand what she was saying until I heard, "Scotty's dead." Scotty was Maida's husband and Jeffrey's best friend from childhood. Although we didn't see them that often there was a deep bond between us all. He was only 26.

I hung up thinking it was a bad dream. Scotty couldn't possibly be dead. We had just spoken to him and Maida earlier that night to make plans for their visit to New York from Dallas. After a moment of lying still, I woke up Jeff. We decided to call Maida back. It was true. Scotty had died in his sleep from heart failure.

We stood in Dallas' Jewish cemetery on one of the hottest

July days on record. The cemetery was as barren as I felt. There wasn't a tree in sight to stand under for relief from the scorching sun. As the rabbi gave Scotty's eulogy, it was impossible to believe we were at his funeral. I kept revisiting the conversation we had with him the night he died. He and Maida and their little one were coming to New York. We went over all of their plans for their upcoming visit. We should all have been in New York City having a blast together. It didn't make sense. As the rabbi spoke, I grabbed onto one of the only things that made sense to me in the last few days. It was a quote, "Our time on earth cannot be measured in days but rather in our deeds."

As they lowered his simple pine box coffin into the parched ground, it hit with a thump, thump, thumppp. They hadn't dug the hole big enough. The grounds people came and shoveled the hole bigger. They tried to lower him into the ground again. Thump, thump, thump. The sound pummeled me like gunfire. My head felt like it was splitting open into two halves, like a pecan being cracked wide open. I felt dizzy and weak and prayed I'd hold it together until the burial was done. The rabbi said the prayer for the dead in Hebrew as they lowered the coffin for the last time into the earth. As Scotty's coffin landed with a huge thumppp, a ray of heat shot through my body. I could no longer sense the ground and prayed my feet would continue to hold me upright.

We bowed our heads for the final moment of silence. A voice declared in my head, "You must live your life now." A deep chill went through my otherwise overheated body. I thought I was living my life. "Whose life am I living if I'm not living my life?" I asked this voice. "And whose voice am I speaking to?"

Scotty's stepdad stepped forward, picked up the shovel and threw dirt onto the coffin. The rabbi began a new prayer over the coffin as each person, one by one, took their turn shoveling dirt. As my turn drew near, the heat seemed to escalate. The voice screamed, "Now you must live your life." Each pebble and rock that hit Scotty's coffin accentuated the message.

After the funeral and sitting Shiva for a few days with Scotty's family in Dallas, we returned to New York, back to our jobs in Manhattan and the daily-ness of our lives. Jeffrey was a tax accountant, the first male in his family not to work in the family business. He was a Newhouse, owners of a media empire, including Conde Nast. I ended up working in the business.

My first position was at Bride's Magazine. Later, through a vigorous and competitive interview process, I succeeded in getting a position on my own merit at Vanity Fair in the sales department. I had been at Vanity Fair for just about a year. It had been quite a coup to actually win the position as New Sales Manager. My coworkers whispered that I had been offered to apply for the position because my last name was Newhouse. In reality, I had had a stellar year in sales at Bride's Magazine that had made it possible for me to interview for the position. I competed against people who had had many more years experience than I in the industry and I believed I won it on my own ingenuity. It didn't hurt that I was married to a Newhouse but at the same time, more was expected of me. I had to prove that I was worthy of the position, name or no name.

My sales started out with a bang, working with Sony, JVC and other Japanese products. During the first two quarters, I thrived on the pace of work, the excitement of winning over these skeptical buyers and filling my quota with ad pages. I quickly became disillusioned with how these Japanese men and their American counterparts treated women in the business. Selling ad pages slowly began to lose its zest and appeal; I longed to make a difference in the world. Though I was successful at sales and loved getting approval from my bosses, I began to wonder what difference it made if I sold one or a hundred more ad pages. If I had needed one more push, Scotty's death provided the fertile ground upon which I debated myself and my life's work.

Returning to my desk at Vanity Fair after Scotty's funeral, I couldn't think about anything except Scotty's death, death in general, the voice at the funeral and what was truly important in life. Even though I'd had people in my life die, Scotty's death touched me in a way that no one else's had. I could've cared less about selling another page of ad space. What had once been a driving force in me now seemed ridiculous. I spent that first week after his funeral shuffling papers from one pile to another.

Almost one month to the day, another death threw me. Mari Jo, a sales rep who sat opposite me, got horrific news that her fiancé died of a heart attack at 42. If I'd been recovering at all from Scotty's death, this news insured that I wouldn't go back to my comfortable state of denial. Looking at Mari Jo's ravaged face as she told us the news, my heart broke apart once again. Something deep inside me was irrevocably shaken awake.

In the weeks that followed, the neat stacks of paper lining my desk grew out of control. The sales calls that once gave me a surge of adrenaline now lived in a bottomless dark hole labeled "insufficient". Each day I promised myself to resolve the pile, as well as the long over-due phone calls. More weeks passed and nothing seemed to get done. At home, I was unusually quiet. Afraid to tell Jeff or anyone else about the voice, afraid to admit that something in me had been altered, I focused on everyday things like laundry and making dinner, while desperately trying to pretend that all was okay.

A few months later, Corey, the new ad director, called me. "Hi Ellen, I'd like to have a chat. Could you come to my office in fifteen?"

"Sure," I tried to be upbeat and override the butterflies in my stomach. I knew what was about to happen. As I approached Corey's office, I heard a warm, "Come on in," and went in and sat in the seat opposite her desk.

Corey got up, closed the door and sat in the seat next to me. She looked chipper. Her perfectly coiffed hair seemed to have more bounce to it.

"How are you doing, Ellen?" she asked.

"Considering many things, I'm fine."

"How do you feel it's been going for you lately?"

"Not so great."

"I've noticed that. Fred has noticed that as well." Fred was the publisher. "I'm afraid it's not been going well at all. Your numbers are really down for the quarter. Ellen, do you really want to be here?"

I sat and thought about the game that was before me. Was she was going to fire me or was I going to fire myself? I knew she'd prefer me to fire myself. Did I have a choice? Up until the last two quarters, my numbers were superb, heroic even. But there were other facts that I wasn't privy to. I wasn't a political player and I had no interest in being one.

Corey was a player. She went for the kill and nailed it. I was no match for her. She always had her game face on. She had a cheery face and full cheeks, and I wondered what she really thought inside.

"Ellen, it's clear that you haven't been here. I'm sorry but this is just not working out," she said.

I took a deep breath. "I see."

Without missing a beat, she said, "So, I've been thinking when we meet with the staff at tomorrow's meeting, you can say that you are leaving to pursue your dreams. How does that sound?"

I had just been fired. "That sounds fine," I said, in shock.

At home, I spent the next several months contemplating my life and myself. I decided to do something just for me every day, not what my father or anyone else wanted for me. It was the hardest thing I'd ever done.

One day, on the corner of 2nd and 46th I asked myself the simple question, "In this moment, just this one moment, what would you like?" I wouldn't allow myself to move until I found an answer. My whole body shook with fear, fear because I didn't know, and fear that I would answer it wrong. But there was no right or wrong answer. There was just an answer. After many moments in silence, a small voice within me said, "I'd like an ice cream, but I can't have that." I wept with both sadness and joy. To be a good daughter, I had learned to deny myself even the simplest things. The communication within myself had shut down to the point where I couldn't hear what I wanted. I walked to an ice cream shop, ordered a cup of coffee ice cream and enjoyed each spoonful. A locked door had flung open.

The idea of studying acting began to bubble up in my consciousness. Although I thought acting was a frivolous pursuit, it persisted. After a few weeks researching studios and teachers, I found a reputable acting studio, The T. Schreiber Studio, interviewed with them and began their training program.

"In order to fully embody the character you wish to portray, you're going to have to give up your smile. We need and want to see all of you," the teacher, Carol, said in one of my first classes.

As I stepped onto the grey stage, she asked, "Do you have an activity prepared for today?"

"Yes, I am going to sew."

"Good, now don't tell us the background. We want to see what this is about. We want to feel the emotion through the sewing activity. Yes?"

I nodded and took my seat in a beaten-up orange painted wooden chair next to an old metal folding table. From my knapsack, I pulled a pack of sewing needles, brown thread and a man's red and brown plaid shirt I'd bought at a thrift store. As I began to sew the rips in the shirt, I fidgeted, smiled a lot and couldn't seem to concentrate on the sewing or on the story I had created for this character. She was sewing a shirt that had belonged to her beloved father who had just died.

Instead, I focused on the hot lights beaming upon me, and my fellow actors staring at me. I wanted to run off the stage, to laugh out loud. I could feel my face flush beet red.

"It's okay for you to show us what's behind your red face," Carol said from the audience.

I began laughing hysterically. Much to my surprise, my laughter turned to tears.

"Good," Carol said, "keep sewing. You can have all your emotions. Just stay in touch with whose shirt it is, what's been going on and what you're actually doing."

Lifting the shirt and inhaling, I infused myself with the father I loved. As I sewed, I laughed and cried, remembering how as a little girl I had picked at the tiny holes in my father's shirts just like the ones I was sewing. We'd made up stories about the holes. One that we had expanded on for years was about a family that was so small that even the human eye could not detect them. They lived inside people's clothes. Sometimes, they would have growth spurts and stretch the clothing until it ripped. These growth spurts were of their brains as much of their physical size. One of my father's shirts had so many holes, he figured at least two families lived there. We named all of the family members and talked about them as though they were real friends.

"Excellent," said Carol, "You left your smile and your point of view and entered into your character's world. Now that's what we're wanting. As you enter that world, you allow us to enter with you. And you did it without your smile, without your mask. Well done."

The smile that had opened many doors for me became my greatest liability in acting. It did not allow me to reveal the truth of a character's emotional reality. My smile that had helped me make it through times when I wanted to scream and protected my true vulnerability from my father, would not serve me here. Over the next few months, I kept a straight face for a few moments longer each time, but each time I felt frightened. Behind my mask were dark feelings of anger, grief, sadness and shame. Afterwards, I'd feel disoriented for days.

I began to have trouble breathing. At first, I got winded easily. Within weeks, I could only take shallow breaths. Within large groups and in enclosed places like taxi cabs and movie theatres, I felt suffocated.

A doctor told me to quit smoking. It was brutally hard, but after a few tries, I conquered cigarettes. He diagnosed me with asthma, but the medication and inhaler he prescribed never helped.

I spent the next year in search of a solution within the western medical model. A dizzying array of medications were prescribed, none of which seemed to help. Neither the doctors nor I linked my breathing issues with the uncovering of my emotions.

No one was sure why I wasn't able to breathe or why none of the medications helped. At my last doctor's appointment, the specialist said, "We really don't know why you are not breathing at a maximum level." All he could do was offer me an oxygen tank. I walked home in a fog.

As I entered our apartment on the upper West side, I felt completely alone. Who could I turn to for help? Too many thoughts surged through my head. Would I suddenly die from this lack of breath? I became paralyzed with fear. Sitting on the bed, looking up at the ceiling, I said, "Listen God, forgive me if I don't know how to pray to you correctly. I need you to get down here and help me now." I started sobbing, "Please I am not ready to die." I waited for a reply. I expected a booming voice to say, "Ellen, God here. Don't worry my dear. I am here."

Nothing like this happened.

Crazy

As my practice of praying developed, I began getting "crazy ideas." These had a different quality from my random thoughts. It was as if someone else was sending the messages. They began as simple concepts: meditate more; call your mother; listen to your heart; go to a talk on yoga; take a yoga class. But they became stranger: meditate for a 24-hour period; do a detox of olive oil, cayenne pepper and fresh lemon juice; don't eat wheat, sugar or dairy; walk more, walk slower; go swing in the park; laugh at life and don't take everything so seriously.

A critical voice wanted me to disregard these voices. "You'll end up crazy like your mother if you start listening to these messages. People will think you're crazy. You are crazy. You've lost it."

Despite the critical voice, I decided to follow these crazy ideas, hoping they'd bring me something or someone who could help me to heal. "Maybe I'm nothin' but a damn fool like you say," I told the critical voice one night at 3 a.m., "and maybe I'll go crazy like you say following these ideas but I'm so sick and tired of struggling to just breathe, I don't care anymore."

I didn't dare share this with anyone. This would be my own private experiment. Few people would have understood or honored me for speaking with unseen voices, let alone for following the ideas that they channeled through me.

One idea was to go to an herb shop. I found one listed in the yellow pages in Greenwich Village. It was one of the old mercantile shops, dusty wooden slat floors that leaned and sloped in different directions and a narrow staircase that went straight down to the storage area in the basement. Large glass jars held herbs of various kinds. I knew nothing about herbs and closed my eyes and prayed, "Dear God, you have sent me here for a reason, show me which herb(s) will help me with my breathing." Suddenly I felt a light tap, tap, tap upon my left hand. I thought I would jump out of my skin.

On the second step of the staircase stood a frail Chinese man. In his best broken English he said, "Sorry, you sick. I help." I wanted to run out of the shop screaming. "In China," he continued, "I use needles. Here use only hands. I help."

How did this old man who'd never laid eyes on me know that I was sick? How was he going to help me with his hands when some of the best doctors in Manhattan couldn't? I was dumbfounded and suspicious but desperate for a solution.

"I give you address. You come here, and I help." He wrote his address on a piece of paper. "You come." He handed me the paper.

I shoved the paper into my coat pocket and left, walking away from the store as fast as I could until I was at a safe distance. I sat on a bench beside a basketball court and pulled the piece of paper out to look at his address. It was way up in Harlem. What had just happened? I felt out of control and frightened. How could this frail man who barely spoke English know he could help me? He looked as though he might just fall over himself. And yet he exuded this calm, knowing confidence. Was he just some kind of quack taking people for fools? I didn't dare share any of this with Jeffrey for fear that he would have me committed for being truly insane. We had both been brought up in families that valued western medicine. Jeff and I had become distant. In my quest to heal, I seemed strange to Jeff and to myself. He and my best friend were already questioning my sanity. I didn't want to give them any more ammunition. I was already questioning my sanity myself.

The following morning I took the fact that I could not get Dr. Wang out of my head as a sign to go for just one appointment. I picked up the phone and put it down at least four or five times before having the courage to call. A woman answered, speaking much better English than Dr. Wang. I made the appointment for the following day at 3. The woman gave me directions by subway and bus. I got a deep chill. "Oh God," I thought, "I'll be lucky to make it up there and back alive." One night, Jeff and I had gotten lost driving in Harlem. Terrified, I convinced him to run every red light. I thought of me, a nice Jewish woman, going up to Harlem on this subway, and decided to take a cab instead.

I left plenty of extra time to be on time. I hated being late for anything. The cab pulled up to an old ornate brick building enclosed by steel gates. Every ounce of my being wanted to tell the cab driver to take me back home. I resisted the urge and got out. There was an intercom and buzzer system to the left of the gates. I buzzed 4C.

"Hello," Dr. Wang said, "Come in." He buzzed me in. There was another buzzer at the front door. The security system exacerbated my jittery state. Inside, a wide marble staircase greeted me. This had once been a smart place, but now the plaster walls were cracked and the off-white paint had grayed. There was a deafening silence marked by the echo of my heels against the stairs. Finally, I stood in front of Dr. Wang's opened door.

"Come in," he said. I scanned the one room. The walls were battleship gray. A large window allowed sunlight to flood the otherwise dull, barren room. An old army-like cot, an old massage table with aluminum legs, a large green blackboard, two schoolhouse chairs and a square oak table sat off to the right. I envisioned this old man raping me or strangling me and resisted every urge to flee.

"Please have a seat." He motioned me to the army cot. "First, I go over the body, and then we'll talk before I treat you. Please lie down on your back and relax."

I muffled hysterical laughter. Relax? Are you kidding me? I smiled at him, lay back and prayed he wouldn't kill me. Much to my surprise, he didn't even touch my body. He kept his hands a few inches above me as he moved them over my body. He was done in less than five minutes.

"Okay, please sit up."

"Oh my God," I thought, "if this was his treatment, the guy's a total scam artist."

"The problem," he stated confidently, "is here." He pointed to my uterus and heart. "The problem is very old."

"Oh, sure," I thought. "This is how he gets women to undress so he can rape them."

"The problem," I said, tearing up, "Is in my lungs. I can't breathe correctly."

"No," he stated emphatically, "The problem is in the uterus and heart causing breathing problems." My mind couldn't grasp his thinking. "Very old. Too much sadness. Please lay back."

"I'm not sad," I said. I tried to relax but thoughts screamed through my head. "Are you kidding me? What kind of bullshit is this guy shoveling out? He doesn't know shit. If the real problem was so old then certainly..."

I was hit by a hot wave rushing through my body, like a shower of heat running through me at a deep level. My body began jerking. The heat stopped and was replaced by a burning in my chest. Silent, hot tears ran down the sides of my cheeks. I took a deeper breath than I had taken in a long time. As I wondered how the hell this man was doing all of this without touching my body, a second wave of heat flooded me. I felt overwhelmed by the energy. My body began moving as if someone had put a paddle on my heart. Just as I thought I couldn't take much more, it stopped. I felt drowsy and dropped off into a deep sleep. When I awoke, Dr. Wang was standing on my right side looking at me with deep compassionate eyes.

"Take a deep breath," he said gently. "Let yourself awaken slowly. Sit up when you are ready."

I sat up too quickly and felt dizzy.

"Slowly," he said. "Please slowly."

When I finally got up, I felt deeply tired and heavy but calmer and more peaceful than I could remember being in a long time, if ever. I also felt utterly confused. What had he done?

"Please, have a seat over here." He pointed to the wooden chairs. "You feel much better now and even better over the next few days," he said, smiling and exposing a gold-capped tooth. "You did very well. You very Chinese." I didn't understand either of his comments. "You should study Qigong. I teach you."

"Okay," I said, knowing I was not going to study with this man. I was more afraid of him than before. I just wanted to get this over and escape from him.

"We meet on Sundays in Riverside Park at noon. You come on Sunday."

"Okay," I lied.

"And you should become Chinese doctor," he said. "You very Chinese. You go to China."

I laughed nervously. "How long would it take to become a Chinese doctor?"

"Five years."

"Sorry," I said, "I'm married." My father had ingrained in me that the only thing a good woman could be was married. Making money was also good.

"Sorry to say, marriage no good. You become Chinese doctor. You be good doctor."

Tears flooded my eyes. The old man's words cut straight through my heart. I had known it for a long time, but didn't want to disappoint my husband and was too afraid to disobey my father. A year earlier, I had gone to talk with my father about my relationship with Jeffrey.

Sitting in the back seat of his old mustard Mercedes, I said, "Dad, I think I need to get a divorce."

"Ellie, no one in our family has ever been divorced or will ever be. Do you understand me? This conversation is now over. Is that clear?"

"Yes." Nothing more was ever mentioned about me getting a divorce.

"You become doctor," Dr. Wang reiterated. "You be good doctor. You have good heart. Please," he said, handing me a crumpled paper bag filled with loose, raw herbs. "Take these two times each day for three days. You make tea with these in water and boil. Follow these directions. Breathing will improve."

The directions sounded simple enough. I did, however, worry about the cleanliness of the used paper bag and thus the herbs. Still, I decided to do what he said. I already felt better and figured it wouldn't hurt to go through with the entire treatment.

"I see you Sunday, yes?"

"Yes," I lied again. "Thank you."

As I sat in the back of the taxi taking me home, I realized

my breathing was much better. I couldn't believe it. All the way back, I kept checking my breathing; it was truly better. I didn't feel the need to suck the air into my lungs. My chest didn't feel so tight.

I made the first batch of tea immediately, so I could drink it before Jeffrey got home. As the tea brewed, I never imagined that anything could smell so strange. It never occurred to me that it might taste as weird as it smelled. The first sip caught me off guard and I spat it into the sink. It was thick and dark and tasted like bitter dirt with a sour, skunk-like aftertaste.

"Oh God, what the hell is in this?"

I pinched my nostrils, poured the tea into my mouth and forced myself to swallow. I did this three more times until the cup was empty.

During the middle of the night, I awoke with an overwhelming urge to vomit. I never vomited. I made it to the bathroom and had explosive bouts of vomiting with uncontrollable crying jags. I shoved a towel under the bathroom door to muffle the noise, and prayed Jeffrey wouldn't wake up. By early morning, it was over. I crawled back into bed and prayed for sleep, dozed off and had violent dreams. When I awoke at 8:30 a.m., I was clammy and weak, my pajamas were damp with sweat. My head felt like a bowling ball. My mind raced through the dreams. As I tried to make sense of them, I fell back to sleep. One hour later, I awoke and felt amazingly better.

The idea of facing two more cups of that evil dirt was daunting. Rather than consulting with Dr. Wang, which would have made sense, I called my therapist. We discussed all the reasons I didn't want to speak with Dr. Wang, my fears of him, the tea and dying. I calmed down and found the courage to stay the course with his herbal treatment.

As I drank as much of the tea as possible, the taste became less assaulting, but I worried it would make me vomit again. That night as I made my way to bed, I became frightened to go to sleep, afraid that I would have the awful nightmares that felt so real. I lay awake for as long as I could.

In the middle of the night, I awoke in what can only be described as real life surrounded by extraordinary circumstances. Or was it a dream within a dream? Four men stood over me in what looked like period clothing, black garments with tall black hats. As odd as they were, they felt familiar to me.

"What are you doing?" I asked.

"You should not have awoken. This is very unusual, highly unusual," said the man facing me.

I watched them massaging my heart.

"Your heart needs to be turned," they said in unison, "so that it may open."

"We will help you open your heart," said the most active man to my left.

"Who are you?"

"We are your guides."

I was never alarmed, feeling only peace and a strong love coming from the four men. I felt safe in their presence.

At 5:17 a.m. I awoke and felt as if I had been hit by a debilitating flu. I had to go to the bathroom, but didn't know if my body would move. As my foot hit the cold tiled bathroom floor, a hot flash of heat spiraled through me followed by a violent burst of diarrhea. I felt enveloped in darkness. The presence of darkness was around and inside of me. I imagined worms crawling through my body. Dark thoughts ran through my mind. Was this what hell felt like? Was this the world my mother seemed pulled down into during her nervous breakdowns? After what seemed like eternity but in reality was just a few minutes, this episode stopped as quickly as it had begun. I felt weak but no longer enveloped in darkness.

Back in bed, I fell into a deep sleep. When I awoke two hours later, my breathing had changed significantly. It felt effortless. I felt normal for the first time in two years. One part of me was pulled to go and study with Dr. Wang in the park, while another part was too scared of what this man knew and how he could change my life. I was not yet ready to have my life overhauled.

I drank the final round of tea and slid easily and deeply into sleep later that afternoon. My dreams moved quickly. I kept finding myself in racing objects: cars, planes, boats, helicopters and odd flying machines. They all moved too quickly, and I kept crashing. Crashing was the only way to stop. Surviving one crash, I'd get into another, faster vehicle. My final crash woke me up in real life. I was in free fall, shivering. I wept through the fear. In order to heal, I had to understand the message of these dreams. In the end, I deduced I was moving too fast and needed to learn how to slow down. Going slow scared the hell out of me.

I never returned to see Dr. Wang. I was too afraid. I never had any more trouble breathing.

Six months later, a visiting teacher to our acting class announced, in her crisp British accent, "If you want to have a breakthrough, go where your greatest fear is." My heart pounded, my throat tightened and my palms began to sweat. I knew exactly what my greatest fear was, had known it for years. It was singing. My stomach twisted like a spinning top. If my stomach could have screamed, it would have shrieked a loud and elongated, "No." But nothing could have stopped me from following through on her suggestion. I was desperate to break through the obstacles that were keeping me from being the talented actress all my teachers said I could be.

By that afternoon, I made an appointment with a music teacher on the upper Westside. My throat continued to feel tight and strained all that day and the next. Even as I went up the old stairwell leading to Gigi's walk-up apartment on the fourth floor, I could feel my throat gripping inside.

Gigi was a tall slender woman in her early thirties with reddish brown hair and blunt bangs that framed her cat-like eyes. "Welcome," she said with a huge and inviting smile. She showed me into the living room, and I took a seat by her piano. She asked me a few questions about my musical history and explained that she first wanted to get an idea of where I was in my singing. I could have told her, absolutely nowhere. I smiled, pretending to be fine, and did my best to listen to her instructions, but it was as if I were receiving her signals through a dense fog of fear.

She sat at the piano and instructed me to use an ah sound to move up the scale. Just as I approached high C, my throat tightened, no sound came through.

"Is there any reason you stopped here?"

"No," I answered, "my body just stopped."

"Okay," she said gently, "just allow yourself to go through the note the next time."

"Sure." I began on an ah sound and went up the scale. On high C my voice halted again. It was as if I had no voice at all.

Gigi smiled but her slanted head told me she was perplexed. "So what do you think is stopping you from singing here?"

"I don't know." I hated not knowing something.

"Are you afraid of your voice cracking?"

"I don't think so."

"Okay, this next time, I want you to just go right through this note. I don't care what happens. If your voice cracks or shakes, just let it be."

Gigi turned back to the piano. "I'll play a little faster. See if you can take a slightly larger breath before you begin. Just breathe, and let whatever sound out that wants to come, alright?"

"Okay." My face was beet red with embarrassment. I took

a deeper breath and prayed. Gigi sped up the tempo. Just as I reached high C, howls came out of my mouth. My body shook. My whole life cracked wide open on that high C.

Gigi walked around from behind the piano, put her hand on my back and led me to a sofa. I couldn't stop shaking. "Take deep breaths," she instructed.

My eyes felt too wide open. I had seen this look too many times in my mother's eyes. I could tell from the look on Gigi's face that I was not okay.

"I'm just going to take a minute to call a friend of mine who I think will be able to be of help to you, Ellen," she said.

I shook my head through my tears. As she talked on the phone in the kitchen, I tried as best I could to navigate this energy ripping through my body. Gigi came back into the living room where I was now pacing. Holding the telephone, she said, "I'd like you to talk with my friend Richard. He's a healer. I think he can help."

I didn't know much about healers, but didn't care who he was as long as he could help. With little pleasantries, he explained what he thought had happened to me. I tried to listen. As he talked, things began to slow back to normal. He explained that I was having a panic attack likely brought on by a triggered memory in my past of a sound similar to a high C. He asked if I had any memory of this.

I was exhausted and didn't want to think. He suggested that I make an appointment with him for the following day, as he was sure that this wasn't finished. He offered me a few suggestions for what to do should my body begin to shake again. I made an appointment for the next day, just in case. I didn't think I'd need it. I thanked him for his help.

As Gigi walked with me down the stairs and out of the apartment, I told myself that I would never have to endure such a violent and terrorizing feeling ever again. I gave Gigi a hug and thanked her several times before I managed to hail a cab and make it back to my apartment. Little did I know that this was just the beginning of a five-year journey of healing.

Late that evening, I awoke in a damp sweat. A pool of sweat had collected between my breasts. It was 11:59 p.m. I had only been sleeping an hour. I sat up, only to feel that racing feeling starting in my chest. "Please God, make this stop." I looked over at my sleeping husband. He looked so peaceful. I would have given anything to be him.

Jeffrey turned over, pulling the covers with him. His movement startled me and brought me back to our bedroom. The walls were covered in shadow lines from the streetlight seeping in through the slits in our blinds. I took a deep breath and looked at the clock. It was 12:35 a.m. The racing in my body seemed to have subsided. I sank down under the covers and looked at the lines across the bedroom wall. As soon as I tried to sleep, a gnawing feeling hit my stomach. Praying I wouldn't throw-up, I yearned for daylight.

For the next two years, my life was filled with episodes of racing energy, racing thoughts and panic attacks. I often re-lived moments of my childhood filled with terror and fear. I was grateful to have a great therapist and wonderful healers to assist me in my healing.

Richard and his wife Ava were the primary healers that I saw at the time. Richard, a Chinese man in his 40s and Ava, a large white woman with big breasts, studied Chinese and Eso-teric healing arts. They both worked with the energy system in the body through their hands. Ava also worked with crystals.

I didn't understand a lot of what Richard and Ava did. They seemed weird and kooky to me. In the beginning, I re-sisted what Richard had to say. In my head, I argued with him constantly. He didn't mince words and what he had to say was often too harsh for me to hear. He told me that my father was cruel and didn't have the right to bear children.

Ava was warmer and gentler. She would have me lie down

on her massage table and soothe my body and spirit with her energy work and earth mama presence. Together they made a great team.

In 1985, alternative healing was not considered cool and while it was on the cutting-edge it was way "out there". Healers were outside the box for me. How could crystals or energy work heal? It all seemed like snake oil to me.

Richard introduced me to Carrie, a young gay woman who practiced Bioenergetic Therapy. I worked with Carrie two days a week, saw Richard weekly for healing sessions and Ava on a monthly basis. I had also begun my own training in Bioenergetic healing as a way to become more facile in my own body. I went on to commit to a two-year program studying structural analysis of the human body and energy work. I never planned to utilize the information as a healer. I just wanted to be a great actress.

Carrie felt my healing would come from going through the events of my history. I resisted reliving my past, arguing that it was pointless.

"Okay, I'll admit I've lived through a difficult childhood," I said to her during one of our sessions in her spacious office in lower Manhattan. "But it's over, right? I just want to move on."

"No," Carrie replied, placing a New York City phone book on the floor in front of me. "You must get your anger out of your body before it eats you alive."

I stared at the thick phone book. I knew what she wanted me to do with it, but it all felt so futile.

"Ellen, let yourself feel the anger you have at your father."

"This feels forced. It's over. I don't see the point."

"Take a deep breath and feel into your legs. Take a deep breath and feel the anger that lives in your body."

My legs suddenly felt weak and shaky.

"You won't hurt him, and you will help yourself a lot.

Think back to how you felt every time he hurt you or your mother."

A few pictures of him screaming with red bulging eyes flashed through my mind's eye. I wanted to run out of her office. I could barely breathe. I didn't want to think about anything. I was terrified to look at the truth of my father in therapy. Carrie didn't allow me to deny the facts.

I took the phone book, and ripped off the front cover. Some force in me grew, and I grabbed a clump of pages and ripped them out. Then I was ripping out another clump, and another, setting off a cascading effect of me shredding pages for the next twenty minutes. Memories of my father wounding my mother, brother and me emotionally and physically flooded my brain. My anger exploded. "How could you? How dare you do that to us," I screamed at him. "You're the piece of shit. Uuh." I grunted where words could not express the depths of my anguish.

I stopped only when my fingers felt swollen and red and curled into the chair sobbing from years of pain.

"Take a deep breath. Notice how you feel in your body. Take another breath. That was excellent work, Ellen. How do you feel?"

"Exhausted. And very, very sad."

"Yes, you have been carrying so much grief and pain in your body for so long. I'm not surprised. Ellen, believe it or not, this is what will set you free from your past and from the terror you keep reliving."

I agreed that I felt calmer than I had in weeks but I wasn't as certain as Carrie that this was the path toward freedom. The depth of sadness I felt sitting there terrified me. There was nothing for me to do but to feel and acknowledge the bottomless pit of pain I had buried within me.

Over the next few years, Carrie had me punch pillows, use rubber batons to strike piles of rubber mats and write enraged letters to my father, letters I would never send. Through guided meditations, she introduced me to my inner children. Inside me was a 3 year old, a 5 year old, an 11 year old and a 13 year old girl, all of whom were so traumatized they never had the chance to receive nourishment and grow up. When the rage and fear lost some of their intensity, I encountered a layer of deep-seated grief. As I released each new layer of pain, I came to know and understand myself and my history better. Would it be enough to one day allow me to forgive my father as Carrie suggested? I often doubted it, but left that possibility open. Intellectually, I believed the past was over, the abuse was over, but clearly my body had suffered and was still suffering from the consequences of his abuse and the trauma. Living in such a constant state of threat had exhausted my adrenal and nervous system. My body would often break down in uncontrollable shaking attacks that terrified me. To try to manage these panic attacks, I also saw another healer, an herbalist named Jean Cash.

In addition to being a channel, Jean did energy bodywork and worked with medicinal herbs. I'd watch Jean move back and forth, stirring the herbal granules with a narrow wooden chopstick that had been smoothed by ancient hands. Like a long willow branch, her body swayed with her wooden bowl of herbs until the formula hit the perfect note, then she'd stop on point, dip her pinky into the mixture and taste it. "Mmm... ah. Done."

I chose to keep much of what I was going through to myself. Jeff and I had become cordial but distant. He thought I was crazy much of the time. I needed the time to heal and sort things out by myself. I wanted Jeff to understand and empathize, but as soon as I would open up, his comments made it clear he didn't understand. I felt judged instead of heard.

Many of the feelings that came up in my herb-tea-induced

dream surfaced during a trip with my parents and Jeff. The trip started out with laughter, sunshine and anticipation. Jeff and I had spent four days with my parents in their home on Cape Cod, and we were going to have a New York City weekend at our place. We got an early start off of the Cape.

I must have dozed off. Almost an hour into the trip, I was awakened by the mean father's voice chiding Jeff.

"What do you mean by that?" my father asked.

Jeffrey, still unaware of all of Dad's tactics, tried answering as if he were talking to a normal person.

"Well, I…"

"Well, I," mimicked my father in a sissy voice, "you know you really are just a little shit, a scared little shit. You think you're so good. Don't ya, you little shit?"

I hit Jeff's leg to get his attention. I shook my head no, and mouthed, "Don't answer him. What happened?"

"What's the matter? Cat got your fuckin' tongue, you little shit?"

"I'm sorry," I mouthed, "I'm so sorry." My heart ached for my husband. It ached for all of us who had ever been subjected to the tirades of this mean, crazy father.

"You're such a pussy, Jeff. Aren't you? You can't even find anything to say in that brilliant fuckin' lawyer brain of yours. Go figure." He spoke as if he was talking to himself.

"Dear God, please," I prayed, "let me get out of this car alive. I beg of you, make him stop this. Please!"

Once my father's evil outbursts began, they took on a life of their own. But there was a good, fun, charismatic Dad, too, the Dad who loved to sing and dance to Diana Ross's greatest hits. He'd sing "Ain't no mountain high enough," to me in his rich sonorous voice when I was a little girl, twirling me around the living room as though nothing else in the universe mattered. This was the Dad who loved me in a bigger than life way. I was his special one; there were no others in these moments.

We would sit at opposite ends of a room and make strange facial and body gestures until we cracked each other up. We'd hold our stomachs, laughing until we cried.

Today, I let my guard down. We had had a wonderful four days at their house on the Cape with no episodes.

"Did you put the heat up, Jack?" screamed this crazy lunatic of a father driving way too fast. "Didn't I tell you not to touch the fucking heat?' My mother knew better than to answer him. She sat quietly twirling her black hair round and round until I thought I might just vomit. "Didn't I tell you... look at me!"

"Dad, come on," I said.

"Ellen, am I talking to you?"

I flipped him my two middle fingers behind his seat. Jeffrey squeezed my arm, and we smiled at each other victoriously. I wondered if he'd actually have the balls to hit my mother or me in front of Jeff. Typically, he'd first throw a punch at my mother and then tell her she deserved it. Suddenly, the car swerved to the left.

"What a fucking asshole," my father screamed. "You stupid fuck-ing ass-hole!" He annunciated each syllable to the man in the car next to us. I prayed he was an undercover cop who would finally make things right.

"He could have killed us. We could have crashed. Did you see that, Ellen? He could have fuckin' killed us!"

As usual, it was always someone else's fault, always everybody else's fault. "Dad, how's the gas?" I asked, desperate for a reprieve.

"Whose driving, me or you?" he screamed a little less loudly now and began to drive a little slower.

My shoulders and neck ached. I looked over at Jeff. He looked weary and sad. "I'm sorry," I whispered in his ear.

Hot tears welled up and slid out the far corners of my eyes. I felt ashamed and embarrassed that he was my father and sorry that Jeffrey had to be subjected to this animal. I was mad at God and the whole universe. Where the hell was he when you most needed him? Ask and you shall receive. What a joke. I put my head back on the worn leather seat and closed my eyes. I couldn't rest. My anger was a wild beast wanting to rip my father apart piece by piece, limb by limb, toenail by toenail until he could feel the pain he inflicted. I found it hard to contain myself. I needed to scream, but that would not have been tolerated.

So I coughed. I coughed until it hurt. I coughed until I might just vomit. Jeffrey looked at me concerned, but my parents didn't seem to notice.

Years of incidents just like this one flooded my mind. I couldn't take it anymore. I was done with all the lies and pretending that everything was okay. There was nothing okay about him or our lives. We were all infected with his poison. I was done. Done pretending. Done forgetting. Done covering it all up.

For the next couple of hours, I decided what I would say to my father, rehearsing scene after scene in my head until we drove up to our apartment building. My stomach sank. My knees felt wobbly and my head fuzzy. I couldn't prepare my mother or my husband for this. When Dad got out of the car to get our suitcases, I followed him.

"Dad," I could barely speak. "Dad, I need to say something to you." My heart ached. I wanted to run away or close my eyes and pretend that nothing had happened. I wanted to stop the words coming out of my mouth. "Dad, unless you can learn to treat people better, I can't have you in my life."

He threw the suitcases down onto the pavement. Without looking at me, he said in a cold, quiet tone, "Go fuck yourself. Fuck you forever!" Jeffrey jumped out of the car. My father got back in the car, slammed the door, and sped off with my frozen mother staring back at me from her side view mirror.

I don't remember seeing our doorman, the elevator, or our front door. I just remember being inside our living room, doubled over, with a searing pain in my chest that made it hard to breathe and even harder to think. It felt like someone had hit me in the stomach full force.

All I could think to do was to go running in the streets of Manhattan on that black evening, in the pouring rain. I ran for hours until the craziness of the pain subsided enough for me to sit still.

A few weeks later, I sent my father a five-page letter. He steamed it open and wrote in thick red magic marker, "Fuck you, forever. Fuck you, forever" on each page. He resealed it and sent it back marked "return to sender." I wouldn't hear from my father or mother for the next two years.

The Gift

"Ellen, it's Mom. Please call me. Dad's in the hospital. He needs to hear from you. Please call me."

In the two years since I had been silenced by my parents, we had not communicated at all, not even a phone call. I knew in my heart as I listened to her message that even though he was only 56, this was the end of his life. I was furious that only now had she called. She never had the courage to go up against him, not even to speak with her own daughter.

I was tired of always having to be the adult. For two days, I prayed to God for an answer. Finally, I found it in my heart to call my mother back.

"Hi Mom, it's…"

"Ellen, it's bad. Dad's really sick. He had a heart attack, and he can't breathe very well. He's got water on his lungs. They don't know what they can do. He's very sick, Ellen. Can you come home?"

"I…"

"Will you please call him? He needs to speak to you."

"What's his number?"

"Does that mean you're gonna call him?"

"I need to think about it."

"Ellen, please. He's sick. He's really sick."

"Mom, just give me some time."

"Okay," she said in a weepy voice. "It will mean so much to him if you call."

I hung up and screamed at the phone, "Just give me a fucking break! Are you fucking kidding me?" I felt crazy and didn't know what to do with all the energy rushing through my body and mind. The one thing I knew for sure was that I wasn't ready to call my father.

I went out for a run. I couldn't get that rainy night two years earlier out of my head, nor the hurt I felt. How could she suddenly expect me to forget all that had happened? How was I supposed to erase two years of being silenced and hurt?

Back at the apartment, the walls felt like they were closing in on me. There was an enormous weight in my chest as if someone were sitting on top of me. "Dear God," I prayed out loud, "please show me what to do."

I tried to sit on the couch in silence but couldn't and began to pace. I was furious and scared at the same time.

"Why should I have to call him?" I yelled out loud. "Why do I always have to be the bigger one? I'm supposed to be the kid here." I wanted an immediate answer. I would have been happy if the walls spoke back to me.

After two days pondering and praying, I knew that I was to call my father. I received the message that somehow I would be given a great gift by calling him. I made sure Jeffrey was around for support if I needed it.

"Hi Dad. It's Ellen."

"For God's sake, do you think I could ever forget your voice?"

"I…"

"Ellen, I need to say something that you need to listen to."

I took a deep breath and waited for him to start screaming at me.

"I'm so sorry for what happened two years ago, and I'm so sorry for being so cruel to you your whole life."

My heart broke wide open. I wailed uncontrollably. My father had never said those three words, "I am sorry" for anything he had done in his entire life.

"Shhh Ellie. Come on now. Don't cry."

I couldn't control the tears or my howling. I thought the entire apartment building would come running. All Jeffrey could do was to look at me with deep compassion. After a few moments, I managed to get myself under control. A few of our neighbors stopped by to make sure everything was okay. Jeffrey explained that I had just found out that my father was dying.

"It's okay now, shhh." His nurturing tone was like a warm blanket around me. "Come on now, Ellie. It's okay now."

I took a deep breath. "Dad what's happened?"

"I had a heart attack. I was getting better until yesterday when I was supposed to be released. I collapsed in the hallway. I couldn't breathe at all. The nurse said I died for a moment, but then I was brought back."

"Well, maybe they won't let you in until you take care of a few things here," I joked.

"You're probably right." It shocked me how soft he was.

"So, what's the prognosis?"

"It's not good. There's not much they can do at this rate. I've pretty much worn my heart out. They'll send me home with some oxygen. That's about all they can do."

"Are you sure?"

"Pretty much."

"When are you going home?"

"As soon as they think I'm stable enough, a few days probably."

"Then I'll plan to come up this weekend with Jeffrey."

"That'll be great. It'll be great to see you, Ellie. I miss you."

"Me too."

"Ellie," he said and paused, "I'm so sorry for everything."

I shook my head. "Thank you," I whispered.

"I'll see you soon, Ellie." He hung up the phone.

As soon as I hung up, I burst out howling. I couldn't believe what I had just heard. I sat on the couch. Jeffrey sat next to me. After a few moments, he asked, "What did he say?"

"He said he was sorry." I burst into tears again.

"That's amazing."

"You know the funny thing is," I laughed, "I think it was a lot easier when he never agreed with me."

I couldn't believe he'd used the word cruel. It caught me off guard. That word pulled back the veil of denial, laying bare the wounds from years of his abuse. The word mean wouldn't have had the same impact. Even in my denial, I could see that at times my dad was mean, but that didn't cut to the bone the way cruel did. Cruel allowed his abuse to be acknowledged and witnessed. Cruel was the gift he handed me, a gift I needed for my complete healing. I would never be able to go back into denial. If I ever questioned what had happened in our house, the word cruel ensured that I held onto the truth.

Even though I raged at my father my entire life, I really didn't want him to agree with me. It was too confrontational, directly challenging the story that I had created to survive. The evil father and the father I adored were two different people.

Even after almost two years of therapy, I didn't know what to do with his admission. To accept it meant that the very fibers of my life would begin to unravel. It would have been much easier to keep fighting rather than to receive the gift that I had just been given.

Over the next few days, I wondered how it would be to see my father. We had both been changed by that phone call. Would he deny saying what he'd said? Was it a momentary lapse into truth telling? Would he be able to hold onto his honesty? What would it be like to look into his eyes now?

I fidgeted with everything and nothing for the four-hour drive to the Cape. When we arrived, I saw him through the living room window sitting with an oxygen tank. Years earlier, I would have been glad to see him hurting or, better yet, dead. But looking at him with tubes in his nose, my heart sank. I took a deep breath, grabbed my bag from the backseat, looked at Jeffrey and headed to the door.

I dropped my bag inside the door. "Hi Dad," I said, reaching down to give him a hug. Normally, I would never think about hugging my Dad. "Well, this kind of sucks." I touched the tube under his chin.

He smiled, but his eyes welled up. "Thanks for coming."

This was not my dad. He was too soft, too transparent. He'd always put on a good front. Only once before, when his mother died, had I seen him this vulnerable.

"How far can you go with this thing?" I asked.

"It gets me around the house."

"That's it?"

"Pretty much."

"Can you get out of the house?"

"I've got a portable one that's pretty good."

"Thank God."

"But I'm not moving very fast as you'll see." He began coughing, choking on mucous. "Don't worry. I sound worse than I feel. Go put your things in the room and say hello to your mother." His face turned burnt red.

As soon as Jeffrey and I closed the bedroom door, I lay on the twin bed, crushed my face into the pillow and burst into tears. It reminded me of so many nights alone in my bedroom. Then, I would never have believed that I would ever be crying because my father was sick and dying.

"Ellen, can I come in?" my mother asked. I shook my

head no to Jeff.

"Sure, come on in," he said.

"Hi Jeffrey. Ellen, thanks for coming."

I sat up on the bed. "Mom, he looks so much older."

"Oh honey, I'm so glad you're here this weekend. You light him up, Ellen."

"Mom, what are we going to do?"

"There's nothing anyone can do. He's just glad to be home."

"What are you going to do?"

"There's nothing for me to do."

"What do you mean there's nothing you can do?"

"Let's talk later. You guys must be starving. Jeff, what do you want to eat?"

"I think a nap would be a good idea first."

"Okay. You guys nap, and we'll eat later." She closed the door behind her.

"Oh my God, is anybody dealing with how sick he is?" I whispered to Jeff. "Do you see how much older he looks?"

"You're right, he looks terrible, but they can only do what they can do."

"What the hell is that supposed to mean?"

"They'll just deal with what's right in front of them. That's all they can do."

I glared at him and slammed my body against the bed. I fell asleep within seconds of hitting the pillow. I always slept a lot when visiting my parents. They thought it was because I was exhausted, but it was my way of coping with being in such close proximity to them.

I awoke with a stir. The room was dark. It was pitch black outside. The clock read 9 p.m. How had I slept so long? My mouth felt like cotton. I sat up quickly and felt dizzy, and lay back down to see if the dizziness would subside. Images of my father, pre-heart attack, flashed through my mind. I realized as if awakening out of a dream that he was now the man attached to an oxygen tank by long plastic tubes. I would have given anything to be fighting with the father I had always fought with, laughed with and loved. It would even have been a relief to hear him screaming about some stupid thing. The clock ticked against a silent house. I tried again to get up, this time more slowly. The dizziness had managed to recede. The house was so quiet I thought maybe they all went out for dinner. I left the bedroom and walked down the hall to the kitchen and den. My father dozed on his brown leather lazy boy chair. My mother and Jeffrey sat in silence watching a movie while my father's oxygen tank hissed. In the stillness my mind drifted off.

"Healer?" I asked, sitting across from a psychic on the lower East side. Usually, you would not have caught me going to a psychic, but I was desperate. Suzanne, an acting friend, had recommended her.

"Yes," she said, "You are to be a healer." She smiled, reached across the table and put her hand on top of mine. "Let me do some breathing and journey work with you so that you can feel what I am talking about." She began by instructing me to breathe deeper into my body.

"Now, let's begin by imagining that there is a large doorway off in the distance. I want you to begin walking towards that door. Now feel the handle on the door and open the door and walk through." She led me on a pathway. As she led me to steps going down, everything accelerated. It was not a comfortable feeling. I felt out of control, like I was on another planet. After trying to be with this feeling a bit and make it alright, I said out loud, "Beth, this is feeling very uncomfortable. Can you bring me back?"

"What are you feeling?"

"I feel like everything has accelerated, and I can hear a

conversation that is taking place where I am."

"Where do you feel you are?"

"I don't know, but I feel scared, and I want this to end."

"Okay," she said and talked me back into my body and back to everyday reality. She asked me about the conversation I seemed to be listening to. All I could tell her was that it was like overhearing a muffled conversation in the next room. I could hear people talking, but couldn't hear what they were saying.

Beth explained that I had gone into what is called Automatic Transmission, a state in which you begin to channel energies from other realms. Despite her excitement, I didn't want to hear about channeling, other energies or other realms. I had witnessed far too much as a kid with my mother fighting demons as she escalated into her psychotic episodes. It was the same reason I mostly stayed away from drugs. I was far too afraid of losing my mind.

Beth gave me water to drink and had me breathe deeply again into my body, especially my feet.

"How are you feeling now?"

"Dizzy and light headed."

She held my feet and did energy work until I felt stable. She reiterated that I needed to do my healing work. I was confounded and didn't understand why she used the phrase, "my healing work". Not only did I not feel called to be a healer, I hated the thought of it. It seemed like such a menial job.

"I believe you are an open channel. It is a great gift."

In my mind, Beth didn't have the gift of listening. Nor could she see how painful this session had been for me. This psychic confirmed my diagnosis of all psychics. They were misguided. Still dizzy, lightheaded and afraid, I paid her and left. No matter what I told myself, I couldn't shake the fear emanating deep within my body. Thinking fresh air would help, I decided to wait and take a bus rather than jump into a taxicab.

Standing at the bus stop, I suddenly felt hot, flushed and too open. That conversation started again off in the distance. Inside my head I said, "No." The conversation seemed to stop, but I still felt as if someone were standing next to me. I managed to breathe down into my feet as Beth had shown me. The heat left as suddenly as it had appeared. I felt more like myself. If this was what it was like to have a healing gift, I didn't want to have anything to do with it.

Over the next four months, Jeffrey and I spent many of our weekends visiting my parents. Despite my desire for everyone to talk about my father dying, little was ever said until the last weekend before he died. My mother doted on him despite the years of abuse.

"This is the perfect opportunity for you to get even with him, you know," I said to her half-jokingly one day in the kitchen.

"I don't need to be mean to him. He's already in incredible pain. He knows what he's done, Ellen, and he needs to live with that now."

He wouldn't even look her in the eyes. I wondered if he ever said he was sorry for being so cruel to her.

Despite his growing awareness, he was still unable to curtail his cruelty.

I had begun studying various aspects of healing, notwithstanding my own initial skepticism. I was even beginning to accept my ability to be a channel.

Jeffrey and I arrived for a weekend visit, my father was sitting in the den. His friends were in the living room. They had been visiting for a while, he grew tired and retreated to the den where he was more comfortable in his reclining chair.

"Hi Dad," I said leaning over him to give him a hug. His

eyes brightened.

"Come sit and tell me what's new."

Over the rhythm of the oxygen tank, I exploded with excitement. "I have been channeling. It's amazing. I can feel the presence of other beings. The energy I feel is amazing, Dad."

"What is this channeling?"

"Basically, the kind that I'm doing is that I open my being to be a conduit for other beings that have information to share with us that can help us to live our lives in an easier fashion. I'm opening up to the divine."

"Would you do this for my friends? I think they might find it very interesting."

Even with his low energy, he managed to yell to his friends that I had something interesting to share. I walked into the living room and greeted them, many of whom I had known for years. "I have been studying channeling for the past year. My teacher feels that I have a great gift for this kind of work, and I'd love to share it with you."

"Sure," said one of his friends, "What the hell. This could be interesting."

"Your head isn't going to spin around, is it?" asked Joe, who went to church regularly.

"No, it isn't anything like that. You'll probably feel a change in the room. The energy will feel more peaceful. Just give me a minute to center myself."

I closed my eyes and turned inward. When I could feel the presence of the energy of the entities, I began to speak, "Welcome, my friends…"

From the den, my father began an evil laugh. "Imagine," he said, "my daughter thinks God speaks to her now. She thinks she is so special that God takes time to speak to her."

He'd set me up again. "Excuse me," I said with tears burning my eyes. I ran to the bedroom, wanting to scream,

"Fuck you. Fuck you forever." We never spoke again about my channeling.

Over the next few months, my father continued to weaken. His breathing became more difficult. He lost his appetite and one hundred pounds. His sadness deepened. On what was to be the last weekend of his life, I decided to see if we could really talk. He spent most of his time in bed that weekend, dozing on and off.

"Dad, you look so sad. Is there anything I can do for you?" I said, sitting next to him on the bed, looking into his eyes.

"Will you look out for Robert for me?" It was as if he had been waiting for me to ask.

"Why don't you just call him yourself and tell him how much you love him."

"I can't."

"It would mean the world to him."

"I can't."

We sat in silence. I kept praying for just the right thing to say.

Throughout my life I had grappled with my father's horrific behavior. At times I was so furious I could barely see straight. Other times I took pity on him. And at other moments, I was so heart-sickened I found it difficult to breathe. When I finally entered therapy, I raged at and about him for five years. Since then I had learned many new spiritual principles that helped me to put our relationship into a broader context. I wanted nothing more than to share this newly acquired knowledge with him in the hopes that he would die more peacefully. I just didn't want to sound preachy to him. I had come to understand, that at least on a soul level, we all choose our parents. Through this lens, I understood that ours was a karmic connection. It allowed me to forgive him without condoning his actions.

Finally, I took his hand. "Dad, no matter what has happened, I want you to know I love you."

Even though I raged at him in therapy, my spirit loved his spirit. With five years of therapy under my belt, I was able to differentiate his essential soul from his cruel actions.

I had met two therapists who couldn't understand my love for my father. As they took notes, I could tell that they thought my love for him was dysfunctional. From the outside looking in, I might have also felt the same. But the truth was that despite all of his horrific actions and behaviors, I loved him. When my father wasn't abusive, he had the ability to make me feel extremely special and loved. With Carrie's guidance, I came to understand that this behavior was also problematic as it set me up to be more vulnerable to his manipulation and abuse. The highest highs were always followed by some of the lowest lows. Layer by layer the "truth" was being laid bare in the therapy process.

As a child when my father was throwing dinner plates across the table, pitching random fits of rage, all I felt was terror. Later, as I explored my father in therapy with Carrie and others, I came to understand that he was a wounded, scared little boy in desperate need of love. I could feel my rage at him and still feel the love that existed between us. Was it my spiritual understanding that allowed me to continue to love him, or an unhealthy love bond that kept me bound to him? Perhaps it was a little bit of both. I had begun to understand that I wasn't alone. Often abuse muddled the issue of love, loyalty and fear, blurring the lines. But as he lay dying, I couldn't deny the fact that I still loved him.

Despite all my best efforts, I too found myself raging at my own husband, in spite of the fact that I had told myself for years that I would never treat another person the way I had been treated. It taught me that until we heal our wounds, our rage and anger will surface under duress. When it does, it's then compounded with shame. Shame will tell us we are not worth loving or worse, not worthy of being alive. I could only just imagine what had happened to my grandmother that allowed her to treat her own son the way she had. I understood at the depths of my being that this was how the generational cycle of abuse continued to plague families. Knowing that I would break this cycle by not bringing children into the world and by continually working to heal my own wounds brought me a great deal of peace most days.

"I want you to love yourself. It's done now. Will you do that?" I said to my father as he lay there in silence.

"It's not that simple."

"Yes, it is."

"I'll work on it, Ellie." His eyes belied his words.

That evening, as Jeffrey and I drove back to New York City, I had a strong impulse to write and grabbed a small notebook and pen out of my bag. My hand wrote faster than I could think.

"What are you writing?"

"I'm not sure," I said, without picking up my pen, "but it seems I need to write this." The words streamed into and through me like radio waves onto the paper. It didn't make much sense, but I knew it was important.

What unfolded was a children's story about a boy star who desperately wanted to come to earth. His parents warned that he would forget that he was a brilliant star. In his youth he couldn't imagine that ever being a possibility. He took his case to the council of Wise Men. They also cautioned him of the perils of earth. Human beings often forget who they are. You will most likely suffer the same fate.

He laughed. "I am one of the brightest stars ever born. It is not possible for me to ever forget who I really am." The Wise Men pleaded with him, but he refused to listen. After much deliberation by his star parents and the council, a vote was taken. Together, they decided to allow him to be sent to earth. He was entrusted to a couple who couldn't bear children of their own.

The boy was prepared for his fall to earth. He was given guidance on how other boys his age would act. He was educated about earthlings, what they were like and how they differed from the Star People. The boy was often in disbelief, thinking the Council was trying to scare him. His parents warned him that no matter how much he might miss them, he would never be able to reverse his decision once he was on earth.

He was given sixty days to make his final decision, and to learn how to lower his brightness so he could fit in with the children of earth. Even though he wavered at moments, he decided that earth looked more fun and challenging. He loved challenges. The Star People were sad, but they knew that they would be able to witness the boy's development from afar. He had been born with a special mission.

Once on earth, the boy tried to fit in with the other boys. Over time, he forgot who he was. The Star People kept sending him signals and messages to remind him, but he couldn't receive them or remember ever being a brilliant star.

I wrote until my hand was cramping. The time flew by. The story still didn't make sense to me. I put my journal aside and rested for the remainder of the trip. We got in late. Exhausted we climbed into bed, leaving our bags unpacked.

The phone rang at 6 a.m.

"Ellen, he's dead. Dad died at 5:15. His heart just gave out." My mother's voice quivered.

"Are you okay?"

"I'm okay. When can you get down here?"

"Tomorrow. Can you get someone to stay with you tonight?"

"Brian will be here."

"Good. Let me call you a bit later." I hung up.

I pulled my journal out of my unpacked bag and read the story. Now it all made sense. It was my father's story. I knew that I would read it at his funeral.

Death

I'd tangle my father's feet in telephone wire at the top of the stairs, give him one good shove and watch him tumble head first down the red carpet. Or I'd sneak under his car and cut his brake line so he'd careen into a telephone pole on Beacon Street. My siblings would hold him down while I ripped him limb from limb. Red Kool-Aid spiked with cyanide, I'd watch as the slick liquid seared his precious throat.

As a teenager, I spent hours plotting ways to kill my father, elaborate plots that scared even me. I'd rehearsed his death so many times, that even after I grew up, I was certain I'd be elated when the day arrived. Just seven days after my thirtieth birthday, he died. It was much more complicated than my teenage self could have ever imagined.

I walked out of Shapiro's funeral parlor into the piercing sun and climbed into the back of the limousine alongside my mother and siblings. I was barely breathing. This was not what I had expected. I wasn't relieved or elated. With months, years to prepare, still, I wasn't ready.

With the exception of her bulbous arthritic fingers twitching, my mother was too still. I slipped my hand on top of hers. It was ice cold. In the vacuous silence, I could feel the love bond that had entwined my father and me. My love was still there as it had always been. It became my greatest liability. Was it the same kind of love force that allowed such an intelligent woman as my mother to be wooed and mystified all the way to the altar?

As my father's sole caretaker for the past few months, my mother had shrunk quite a lot. Her shallow breath made me wonder what she was thinking. I remembered the rule we kids made up when we were little. You couldn't breathe or swallow until we passed the cemetery or else you'd die.

"You don't think we all laughed too much during the service do you?" she blurted. Without waiting for an answer, she continued, "I don't think anyone could understand." My family had a twisted sense of humor. When all else failed, we laughed. I looked into my mother's eyes searching for clues. Would my father's death drive her into another breakdown? "No, I'm sure they couldn't," I assured her. She raised her right eyebrow, curled her lip and shook her head. A silent agreement.

The world seemed too quiet. Even the trees we passed, standing upright in full summer bloom, were too still. Normally, I'd have the windows down, drinking in the scent of the warm summer air, but on that day everything smelled stale.

As we pulled in through the black wrought iron gates of the Sharon Memorial cemetery, my stomach sank. Wanting to bolt, I looked over at my mother. With her head down, twirling her short thick brown hair, she looked like a little girl who had just been scolded. She was more daughter than mother. As crazy as it seemed, I longed for one of my father's bear hugs.

Hand in hand, my mother and I walked to the gravesite. The sight of the perfectly straight rows of white wooden chairs made my knees wobbly. The sterling Mr. Kravitz smiled at me, squeezing my hand as he filed past. As my dad's favorite among his cadre of lawyers, Mr. Kravitz was always the first person he called when he got into trouble. When he was put in jail for delinquent parking tickets or for writing bad checks, when the FBI left our house after interrogating my father for five hours about his connections to the Mafia, it was Mr. Kravitz he summoned. Six months before he died, it was Mr. Kravitz who informed him that this time he'd most likely have to do jail time.

Considering how Dad treated even his closest friends, I was surprised at the packed house — everyone from a retired judge to local fishmongers to a few men in pin-striped suits I had never laid eyes on.

My mother leaned toward me and whispered, "Your father would have been so pleased. He always worried about who would come to his funeral. I'd tell him, 'Lenny what difference does it make, you won't be there.'" I smiled. I understood my father's compulsion. Thinking about who would come to my funeral had been a guilty pleasure of mine for years.

Even though the "funny fat man," as the men at Haymarket Square loved to call Dad, was wildly popular, he screwed most of the funeral crowd out of money. If they had come in hopes of getting paid back, surely they knew the line was too long and the coffers empty.

I forced myself to stare straight ahead at my father's casket. "Thank God you lost 100 pounds before you died. I don't know what we would have buried you in otherwise." My mind raced with thoughts about his shoes. I prayed they'd buried him in a newer pair, brown not black, and they had shined them and tied the laces tightly. It always scared me when his laces were untied. I knew I wouldn't be able to break his fall. At 365 pounds, the fall would be hard and possibly fatal.

As a kid, I'd doodle pictures of men's faces in my journals, I'd always split them down the middle: one side happy, the other sinister. I didn't know then that I was drawing my father.

As I got a little older, I dubbed the horrific part, "The Evil Father," the one who never apologized for anything.

Sitting on my right, closer to the edge of the canopy, my elegant Aunt Louisa, who still dyed her hair blond, held a white cotton hankie with lace trim in her long, slender hand. Her sniffling burrowed deep within my being. I couldn't help thinking: "If you really cared that much, why didn't you help him when he was alive?" My father always stood by her. He once even wrote her a check for $50,000. Years later, he retained a famous lawyer to get her doctor husband off of criminal charges. She never gave him his due. He was always, Lenny, the gunif. And she, Louisa, the royal princess, always a step above.

I looked over at my brothers and sister. The baby of our family, Brian, kept picking up his tie and smoothing it down over his belly just the way my father would. He was far more transparent than my dad. Jessa, barely able to contain her emotions, continued to hold my father up on a high pedestal. She couldn't allow herself to see the truth of our father. She embellished his good parts, making his death a far greater loss. Michael sat quietly with his wife next to him. His drawn face revealed the weariness he refused to address. My older brother, Robert, sat at the very end of the aisle in his own universe. He and my father never spoke before his death. The unspoken truths and pain lingered in my brother's ravished spirit.

We all stood together, yet almost as strangers, for the final prayer. I took a deep breath, walked to my father's casket, bent down, scooped up a handful of dirt and threw it on his casket. The hidden pebbles and rock hit with a ding, ding, thump.

Following Jewish tradition, we returned to my parents' house to sit Shiva for the remainder of the week. Strange women busied themselves arranging large platters of dark, earthy, dank chopped liver, garlicky salami, chopped vegetables and overly vinegary potato salad, all of it cold and lifeless.

It was odd to be in the house without my father running the show. I was grateful the door to my parent's bedroom was closed. My mother managed to remain calm but too quiet. I wondered when she'd crack.

Despite my exhaustion and lack of interest in our guests, I sat for hours in the living room listening to them reminisce about my father and his life. We hardly ever sat in this room when my Dad was alive. The furniture seemed unfamiliar. Although it wasn't covered in the thick plastic of my grandparent's furniture I'd stick to as a kid, it had that same preserved feeling.

Brian, the baby of our family, came over and handed me a gold coin.

"What's this?"

"A memento of Dad. I had one made for each of us. "

I cracked up and turned the gold coin over and over in my hand, thinking of how much money meant to my Dad. "Yup, perfect. Thanks."

A red cardinal sat on the window sill outside. It barely moved. Dad loved red cardinals. "You can't stand not being here, huh?"

The last guest left at 7 p.m. I kicked my shoes off and stretched out on the sofa, covered myself with the woolen blanket my sister always said was too itchy and took a deep breath. I couldn't wait to crawl into bed but also wanted to spend some time alone just with our family.

In her crumpled navy blue dress, my mother looked like she hadn't slept in days. But she was still holding her own. For how long? I was scared for her. She had never lived on her own or supported herself.

Michael stretched out on the opposite chair. Brian lay on the floor. Jessa went and got my mother a glass of water. My eldest brother Robert, looking about fifty pounds too heavy, sat on the carpet. He asked, "Ma, what did Dad leave?"

"Robert, there's nothing left."

"What the fuck do you mean? What about the hotels?"

My father had owned two hotels. One housed homeless people that the state paid for. The other was for business people, young families, small conferences and a place to get a good lunch.

"Robert, what the fuck did you expect?" Michael, the middle child, cracked up. "It's Dad we're talking about. I went over the books. He was in the red for years."

Brian added, "The gold coins are all there is."

Robert stood and lunged at Michael. "You fucking asshole, you probably fixed the books." He turned towards my mother. "Ma, you stole what was mine. I gave everything. Whenever Dad asked for help, I fucking gave him everything I had. I had money coming to me. You took what was mine." He bawled like a little boy, snot running down his upper and lower lips.

My mother put her head in her hands. "Robert, stop, stop, there's nothing left. No one took…"

"Ma, so help me God, you'll never see me again." He drew his right arm back and whipped the gold coin in my mother's direction.

Brian jumped to his feet and got in Robert's face. "You fucking hurt her, and I'll kill you. Do you hear me?"

"Stop it. Stop it!" my mother yelled. "I can't take this."

Robert stormed out of the living room blubbering. He grabbed his suitcase and clothes from the back bedroom he'd been sleeping in. "Fuck you all," he yelled as he stomped out of the house, slamming the back door.

My mother held her head in her hands. "I can't take much more of this."

"Mom, just let him go," I said gently. "He'll be fine. He's just upset about Dad. He'll be okay."

"He's not okay, Ellen. None of this is okay."

Rebirth

After returning home to our apartment on the upper Westside from sitting shiva at my parent's home, I felt like a nomad. I'd leave our apartment on 86th and Broadway with no clue as to what I was doing or where I was going. Every mile or so, I'd pick up an item that called to me, a rock, a chip of cement, a feather. I'd never been one for collecting. The whole process seemed odd to me, and I seemed odd to myself: spacey, undirected, and singular.

After each walk, I'd lay the items out on the coffee table in front of me and listen to the answering machine.

"Hi Ellen, it's Tracy. I'm just checking in on you. Give me a call when you can."

"Ellen, it's Stephanie. No rush, call when you can."

I had no interest in calling anyone back. Even though a part of me was relieved by my father's death, I felt alone and disjointed without him. Running the feather across my face, I thought, "Why Dad? Why did it have to be this way? What are we going to do with Mom?"

The turquoise stone I'd found near Greenwich Village

calmed me. I rolled the smooth rock in my hand for what seemed like hours. The answering machine beeped.

"Hi Ellen, it's Laudi. We've all been wondering how you are doing. Call me, okay? I'd love to talk."

Laudi was about the only person who I thought might understand. She'd lost her father when she was in high school. Still, I couldn't bring myself to call her.

On one of my daily walks, I was drawn to a shop that carried fine handmade papers of varying lengths, colors and textures. I was lured by a large piece called Fleuri, rose petals, stems and bits of other flowers were imbedded into the paper. Why the hell was I buying this oversized piece of paper? It was as if I was standing outside watching myself take walks to nowhere and buy paper I would never have otherwise bought, especially without knowing why I was buying it. I was seriously concerned about myself. Would I ever return to the person I was before my father died, an ambitious woman who always had a plan?

I brought the paper home, grabbed the box of collected items and laid them out one by one on the dining room table, a rock, a turquoise stone, a piece of cement, a feather, a Barbie arm, a green rubber band, a silver ring, a chestnut, bark, a leaf, twisted metal, a branch, a bottle cap, a penny, a shell, a red rock, pine needles, pebbles, worn green glass, a piece of a sign with an arrow, and a torn white cloth. I picked up each piece, studied it, and thought about my dad.

Without much awareness, I placed the found objects on the paper. These insignificant objects began to find their perfect place. Within a few hours, they'd morphed into a circle that lent itself to the idea of a tree and the concept of completion. After sitting with it for a day, I realized it was perfect and glued the pieces to the paper, sewing a few that were too heavy to glue. I called it the "Tree of Life".

Jeff and I were astounded by its beauty and the story it

told, especially since I wasn't an artist. Light emerging from darkness. Love emanating from struggle.

In spite of its size and three-dimensionality, we agreed it deserved to be framed. The framer suggested a custom Plexiglas box. Even though it was pricey, we knew it was worth it. It was in memory of my father, the girl I had been, the struggles I had overcome and the woman I was becoming. Jeffrey loved it so much he thought it would be great in our bedroom. We hung it over our bed. With my father now deceased, I was free to express my voice and spirit.

Despite this new sense of freedom, I still didn't feel any direction. Out of sheer frustration, I asked around again for the name of a gifted psychic. One of my acting buddies, Suzanne, suggested a woman named Samantha, an astrologer who was gifted at figuring out a person's talents. I had misgivings about going to another psychic. I prayed my experience would be better than the first one. My judgments about healing had been easing even before my father's death. Still, old, dark familial feelings of negativity continued to bubble up about psychics and the psychic realm.

The linoleum steps leading up to Samantha's walk-up apartment were old, cracked and peeling. "Why do these psychics live like this?" I thought. "If they're so psychic, couldn't they figure out how to make money?"

"Hello," Samantha said in a rich, calming voice as she opened the door. She was petite, with large breasts. "I'm glad you had no trouble finding me. Come in." The apartment was tiny and cozy. A cat sat on the kitchen chair and another lay on top of the refrigerator. I was allergic to cats, but decided not to say anything and wait to see if they bothered me. Without a word, Samantha put the cats in another room and closed the door. Perhaps she really was psychic after all. She poured me a glass of water and showed me to the living room where her built-in bookcases overflowed with books on varying subjects. She clearly loved to read. She was not at all what I expected. She brought a thick book called The Ephemeris to the area where we were sitting and an astrology chart that she had hand drawn.

"Shall we get started? I'll go through each of these houses, and then you can ask me questions."

"Great," I managed to smile even though I was still leery.

She told me that my childhood had been extremely difficult, that my father seemed to overshadow everything in my world. He took advantage of the fact that my love for him was so incredibly strong. "Your mother was very critical and overpowering," she said, pointing to one of the houses on the chart.

"My mother?" I asked incredulously.

"Absolutely. She used her criticism as a way to control everyone and everything around her."

"Are you sure you used my correct birth date for this reading?"

"Yes." My face turned beet red.

"You have this all wrong. You don't have my mother correct at all. My mother was never overpowering. She didn't have any power at all."

"Perhaps," she said a little softer, "perhaps you have needed to see her in a different light. All I can tell you is that what I see in your chart would suggest that your mother was an overwhelming figure in your life. Let's move on, and we can come back to this issue at the end of the reading if it still doesn't make any sense, shall we?"

I wanted to bolt. I couldn't believe I had paid this woman. The more she shared her thoughts about my mother, the more upset I became. She continued talking, I tried to compose myself. I listened through the fog of my emotional uproar until I managed to bring myself fully present. We went through all the houses of my astrological chart. I wanted to be told what I was supposed to do with my life. She kept yammering on about my history. There was too much information to assimilate. I was grateful she was recording the session.

"At this juncture," she said, "being a healer would be the best avenue for the expression of your talents."

"What makes you think that?"

"With Pluto conjuncting Venus in your fourth house of home, it would say you have had many lifetimes, including this one, where you were not supported. And by using your healing gifts, you empower yourself and thereby garner wonderful support."

My heart raced. I took a gulp of water. "And what makes you think I have healing gifts?"

"As a Cancer, your greatest gift is the capacity to feel and to bring that gift to others with great compassion. As you do, you not only heal others but more importantly, you heal yourself. Ellen, you need to do your healing work, or I'm afraid you will continue to get even sicker than you have been."

That was it. I was rip-roaring pissed and in no mood to be polite about it.

"How can you say that?" I exploded. "Do you have any idea how sick I've been? Plus if I was to be this great healer, don't you think I'd already know this?" I crumbled into tears.

She sat with me as I cried out my frustration. In the end, she suggested that I study the tarot with her as a way to become more comfortable with my healing gifts. Despite my exasperation, something in me knew that she would be a great teacher for me. I agreed to begin a private class the following week.

At my first tarot class, I was less belligerent, but still resistant. We discussed tarot, psychic channeling, life, death, spirit, God, relationships. Nothing was too sacred. Samantha continued to persuade me to begin a healing practice. I insisted that I was not yet ready. I was too raw and too much of a mess. And I had no idea how a person would set out to build a private practice. It all seemed mysterious and vague to me. I couldn't even conceive of what a healing practice would look like.

On the subway platform, the high-pitched squeal of brakes echoed against the soot-coated ceramic walls. The E train turned around the bend and shot into the station. "Clank, err, clank, clank, screech!" The glare of the fluorescent lights seemed to pull the echo deep into my ears and into my veins, which were already throbbing from adrenalin. The thick summer heat of August in New York City was suffocating. I was nearly 31 years old, but felt like a little girl of five, ten, fifteen. Despite my desire to run, I couldn't move. Everything was moving too fast and in slow motion at the same time. Dizzy, I feared I'd pass out. Every sound sunk deeper until I thought I'd lose my mind.

I couldn't seem to decide if I should try to make it to my therapist's office downtown or run back to my apartment just two blocks from the station.

"All you have to do is to make it up those stairs and run as fast as you can. Two blocks, and you'll be home," I tried to reason with myself. Another subway pulled into the station packed with people. My chest ached as though someone twice my size was sitting on top of me. No matter what went through my brain, my body wouldn't move. People pushed past. A tall dark haired woman dressed in black pumps, tight black skirt and overly sweet perfume practically ran me over. "Oh, for God's sake," she said as she pushed past. My blood pumped even harder through my veins. My heart beat faster in my eardrums, drowning out the squeal of the trains. Thin lines of sweat ran down the back of my neck and sides of my temple.

My eyes darted back and forth like a wild animal in a cage. "I've got to get out of here," I thought. "You can do this Elle. You can do this."

Another round of terror jolted through my body like a bolt of lightning. I burst into tears and crouched down. Men in blue suits with polished black shoes moved rapidly against the cement while young female professionals be-bopped past me in sneakers. A group of young black men half dancing, half singing shuffled past. One old man with black suspenders, a soft pouch of a belly and thick white hair turned soft worn eyes on me and asked if I was alright. "Yeah, I'm fine," I lied.

Another E train squealed into the station. I could not bear another sound. My head spun. I tried to breathe. Desperate, I reached for a crumpled piece of paper with my list of phone numbers, managed to push myself up from the crouching position and ran towards the nearest payphone on jittery, stiff legs. I prayed Samantha would be there. As soon as I heard her voice, I burst into tears. "I'm scared. I'm so scared. I don't think I can make it through this."

The noise of the people rushing through the station, the oversized old fans blowing air and the squealing subways drowned out Samantha's response. It didn't matter. Just having her on the other end of the line helped me calm down.

"Elle, you're gonna be okay. I promise."

The sounds were no longer deafening. Each squeal of the subway no longer felt as if someone were torturing me, sending electrical impulses surging through my body. Breath made its way into my throat and lungs.

"Elle, are you still there?"

"Yeah, I'm here."

"Do you want to stop by?"

"I think I'm going to try and make it down to Carrie's office."

"Good. Elle, you're going to be fine," Samantha reassured me. "You're going to be fine."

"I hope so."

"I know so. Call me later, and let me know how you are."

"Okay, thanks, Samantha."

I crossed my arms, held my bag tightly against my chest

and went back to the subway platform. I prayed an E train would come quickly and not give me a chance to back out.

When the next E train arrived, I got on and grabbed hold of the metal pole in the middle of the car. There were plenty of seats available but holding onto the pole felt safer. The act somehow grounded me in reality. A thin black woman with huge round eyes shot a smile at me as if she could feel how scared I was. I summoned a shy smile back at her.

With the panic attacks occurring so frequently and randomly, I knew I wasn't stable enough to hold a healing space for anyone else. They struck in enclosed places, subway stations, buses and taxi cabs. But they could ensue any place, any time and for no apparent reason. Their randomness made them more frightening. I was at their mercy. Even though they happened inside of my own body, I had no control over them. Couldn't Samantha see that I had too much terror in me to become a healer? I was terrified I would somehow get lost, lose myself or worse forget who I was. Death would have been far easier. At least in death, there would be finality to the pain and anguish. I wondered if this was how my mother felt.

It wasn't until a few years later when I came across the book *Spiritual Emergency* that I made sense of the attacks. They were another opening in my spiritual awakening. The book differentiated between spiritual events and purely psychological crises. It also discussed how under the mainstream Western medical model there was no room to accommodate or acknowledge the fact that spiritual crises exist and are not a mental illness and shouldn't be diagnosed or treated as such.

Around this time, Jane Wagner's play, "The Search for Intelligent Signs in the Universe," was brilliantly delivered by Lilly Tomlin on Broadway. I was fortunate enough to be there during opening week. Tomlin's creation of Trudy, the not-so-mad bag lady, was riveting. I couldn't help but feel a communion with her. I often felt like Trudy's experience of herself in the world as being "out there on the cutting edge of quantum uncertainty, grappling with the imponderables" resonated deeply within me. Like Trudy, I was in the midst of having a breakthrough, not a breakdown, I just didn't know it. Most days, I thought for sure I was on my way to a complete nervous breakdown like my mother. In sharp contrast to Trudy who was quite comfortable with her friends in high places, notably alien visitors who had chosen her as their tour guide on this "planet in puberty", I was on edge, uncomfortable with the unseen guides who wanted me to be their constant companion. Not understanding what was happening to me was one of the worst aspects of that year. Despite assurances about new medications from my therapist, I refused to be medicated. I had witnessed what they had done to my mother. In lieu of any antidepressants, I chose alternative treatments: bodywork, herbs and running.

Jean Cash, who gave me bodywork for the attacks, was forever telling me that her guides had information for me. Trudy was much more amenable to her aliens than I was to the idea of Jean's guides. It felt like a lot of hooey, woowee. I wasn't particularly interested in the New Age movement. I just wanted to heal and get on with my life. Despite my resistance, I always did what her guides suggested, in the hope of feeling better and healing as quickly as possible.

One afternoon, Jean announced that I needed to meet a brown lady. I cracked up. "So you want me to go stand on Broadway and wait for a brown lady?"

"No, you need to go and meet a woman from India I have heard about." She told me she didn't need to meet the woman, but I did. I was annoyed at her certainty. Due to my desire to heal, I agreed to meet her later that evening. Jeffrey accompanied me. When we arrived at the church hall, a man in orange garb walked toward us.

"Welcome. Amma will be greeting people over there in that room," he said, pointing to our left. "Amma gives darshan in the form of a hug. If you'd like to receive a hug, you can join the line once it forms. Otherwise, you're welcome to sit in the seats. Do you have any questions?"

My head swirled with too many thoughts, strange sensations, smells and words I didn't recognize. "What does darshan mean?"

"It means she gives her blessing to you in the form of a hug."

The word hug was about the only thing I could hold onto.

Indian men in orange garbs, Hindu and western women in white saris swarmed the hall. I found the white women offensive. It felt as if they were parading around announcing how pure, spiritual, and perfect they were. People seemed nice but odd to me. I caught sight of Jean walking toward us. She was dressed in her regular everyday clothes like me.

"I saved you both a seat."

Jeffrey and I followed her as I stared at the sea of colors swirling about, orange, red, white and more white flowing about the room.

As I sat down, I noticed a chair adorned with fresh flowers placed on the pulpit. People began sitting on the floor in front of the chair. I whispered to Jeffrey, "Are you going to get a hug?" He shook his head no.

Jean overheard me. "Ellen, you should get a hug."

"Are you?"

"We'll see, but you should. It'll help."

I looked at Jeffrey. He scrunched up his shoulders and said, "It's totally up to you. Do it if you want to."

I loved hugs, so I thought, "Why not? What harm could a hug do?" I caught sight of another person in orange, and my stomach flip-flopped. My parents' admonishments about the Hare Krishnas came back to me. I leaned over to Jean. "Do you think she could brainwash me?"

Jean cracked up. "Oh my God, no. There's no brainwashing here."

Amma flowed into the room in a white sari and took her seat in the chair. She was young and old all at the same time. Her smile put me at ease. Although the room was dark, she seemed lit up. I decided to get in the line. Jean smiled at me as I made my way down the aisle. The moment I sat down and joined the others on the floor, I felt a strange sensation in my chest. As I moved forward in the line, the sensation grew until I could barely breathe.

My heart began pounding. I kneeled before Amma as her assistant had instructed. As she enveloped me in her hug, my head smacked up against her breast. I was transported beyond time and space. Her hug seemed to last for both seconds and infinity. As she released me, she smiled deeply into my eyes and chuckled. I shook at my core. I managed to walk back to my seat. Everyone was beaming at me. I felt confused and off-kilter.

"How do you feel?" Jeffrey asked.

"Shaky."

"You okay?"

"I don't know."

"She'll be fine," Jean offered. "It's just a lot more energy than she's used to. But it's good. It's really good. It'll help you. You'll see."

Jeffrey looked worried. I felt scared. Everything inside of me was shaking. A tall, thin white woman in a white sari approached me. "It will help if you breathe deeper." I suddenly had the urge to bolt, and told Jeffrey I wanted to go home.

As we walked home, Jeffrey kept looking at me and saying, "I'm sure glad I didn't get a hug. That was a good choice."

His humor wasn't funny. I knew he was trying to make light of what I was going through, but I felt out of control. The worst part was that I had no context to understand what was happening and no language to express it. Nothing had prepared me for the Shakti energy I experienced through Amma's blessing that evening. I later learned that Shakti is the divine feminine creative power, sometimes referred to as The Great Divine Mother in Hinduism. At the time, I only knew that my circuits had been blown. As we walked home, I had an inkling that my life would never be the same.

Even though Amma scared me, I went to see her every year when she returned to the United States for her yearly visits. I never referred to her as my teacher to anyone, not even to myself. The whole idea of guru scared the hell out of me. Many gurus had turned out to be as fallible as I was and worse, womanizers, abusers and users. I didn't want to be conned. My issues with my mother left me with no trust or faith in women.

Years later, I discovered that in Hindi, Amma means mother. When I realized that, it made sense that I was both afraid of her and desperately drawn to her. One part of me longed to be near Mother, while another part was afraid of being captured by her.

I continued to work with Richard, Ava and Carrie. I searched for any tools that could help me during the panic attacks. With Carrie, I continued to unearth buried emotions that now flooded through me. Through Richard and Ava, I began to discover the spiritual aspects of the panic attacks. Whether I liked it or not, I was told that I was a channel for spiritual information and that the opening I was experiencing would allow my guides to work with me as a healer.

I became more open to the idea of becoming a healer. I was chosen to take part in a two-year certificate program for advanced students. Only six people were selected to participate. A chiropractic and osteopathic doctor led the course. We studied the physiological structures, as well as the energy patterns and emotional constructs in human beings. It was very hands-on. We all worked on our own issues in the course. As we released physiological patterns held in our bodies, emotions were released. It was amazing to experience how emotions are held in the body through muscular patterning that eventually becomes so ingrained, we no longer identify it as a pattern of holding. Six months into the program, we began to see the patterns of habitual holding within each other. At the end of the first year, most of us could identify our own patterns. As our old scaffolding softened, façades shifted, and far more vulnerable human beings were exposed. I began to understand the sacred journey we agree to when we work with another. Every time I placed my hands on a classmate, I felt a deep personal responsibility to that person's entire being, not just their physical body but their emotional, psychic and spiritual essence.

In the midst of my studies, Samantha called one Thursday afternoon and asked me if I would be willing to help a young woman she knew. She was severely depressed, fearful, and suicidal despite being on antidepressants. Samantha told me that Donna was in many ways still a child herself and not functioning well as a mom to a 4-year-old girl. My heart sank for her and ached for her daughter. Even though I didn't feel ready to be a professional healer, I felt compelled to work with Donna. I couldn't see then that Donna and her daughter were in many ways a mirror image of my relationship with my mother. With Samantha's encouragement, I agreed to speak with her.

As I spoke to Donna over the phone the next day, I could hear the sadness and despair in her voice. I agreed to work with her once I cleared it with her therapist and psychiatrist, certain both of these professionals wouldn't agree, as I had no degrees to validate my work. I would then be off the hook with Samantha, Donna and myself. Despite my urge to work with her, I still was too scared to embrace myself as healer. Much to my shock, both professionals agreed to let me work with her.

After hanging up with Donna's therapist, I wept with confusion. Why did everyone think that I could help her? I still felt too immersed in my own grieving and healing process, not to mention panic attacks, to be of help to anyone else.

Despite my great resistance, I set up my first appointment with Donna on a Wednesday afternoon. In the back room of the apartment, I set up the massage table I bought at the end of my last training intensive in Polarity Therapy.

Before Donna arrived, I went into the back room and sat in the chair, closed my eyes and prayed. "Dear God, I am doing what I believe you are asking me to do. Please assist me in helping this woman and her child. Please direct me during this session. Thank you."

When Donna arrived, I led her down the hallway, showed her the bathroom on the way and offered to take her coat. "No thanks, I need to warm up a bit." It was a warm sunny fall day outside. I knew the cold she felt was from her deep terror.

"Donna," I asked gently, "could you tell me a little about what you think is causing the depression and overwhelming fear in you?"

"I'm not sure," she answered in a soft, child-like voice, "I thought that's what you could tell me."

"Tell me about your daughter. Does she look like you?"

"I hope not."

"Why not?" I asked. "She'd clearly be very pretty."

"I don't want her to be like me at all. I don't want her to feel like me or act like me. I'm a mess."

"What's a mess?"

"Everything, just about everything," she said with daggers in her eyes.

"Is there anything that's not a mess?"

"My daughter," she said quickly. "She's smart, beautiful and very sweet."

"It sounds to me like she's gotten at least some of her

mother in her."

Donna curled up in the chair into a fetal position and began to weep. "I can't feel like this for the rest of my life. I'd rather be dead."

"Can you tell me what it feels like inside of you right now?"

Donna stopped and looked at me puzzled. "Don't you care that I'm really, really sad?"

"Yes, I care a lot, that's why I really want to know what you feel like inside your body."

"What does my body have to do with any of this?"

"From my point of view, your emotions are held inside your body until they're released."

"No one's ever said that before. How can I release them?"

"That is what I can help you to do with energy work."

"Won't that make me feel worse? I can't feel any worse than I feel."

"At moments you may feel as bad as you do for a little while, but it will pass, and you'll be amazed at how much better you'll feel."

"Are you sure?"

"Yes," I said with a certainty that surprised me.

"Okay, how can we do this?"

"Well, in some way you have already begun to do the work, and now we can add the bodywork part. Are you ready?"

"I hope so."

"Let's start with you lying on the massage table on your back and your head closest to me."

I could sense the old energy that was stuck in Donna's body, particularly in her chest and pelvic area, but I knew I could not start there. It would be too difficult. I began by cradling her neck. Within moments, Donna exploded into howling screams. Without asking questions, I held the space for her to scream and begin to let go of the pain. I followed the energy for the next thirty minutes without judging what was happening.

As she calmed down, we began to talk. She told me about the pain and hurt of her early childhood. I had also received information during the healing, but didn't speak of this for fear of overwhelming her. Mostly, I listened.

At the end of the hour and a half, I discovered how much I actually knew about healing and how guided I was during my work. I knew I would be able to help her. Elated, overwhelmed and uncertain, I committed to working with Donna until she was free of her depression and fear or until she terminated her work with me.

Donna had become my first patient.

That evening as I lay my head down on my pillow, I was overcome with gratitude to all the people, both seen and unseen, who had helped me to begin this path of healing. Despite my judgments, my fear of getting my mother's mental illness and my father's judgments, I loved doing healing work. I felt enormous fulfillment in watching Donna make the connections in herself that would help to set her free from the imprisonment she had felt for most of her life. I was sold. Kicking and screaming, I had begun a healing practice.

Even though I often felt too emotionally raw and not at all ready, clients kept showing up. How could I help facilitate healing for others while I was going through so much of my own healing process? The universe and my guides had other plans. Even if I were only a half a step ahead of someone, I learned I could help them. And I wasn't the one doing the healing. I was the vehicle through which the healing was facilitated. But this could only be understood as my awareness deepened and my ego surrendered.

In the beginning, Samantha referred most of the patients. I met with them in the small back room in the apartment. Soon, patients began referring friends, bosses, co-workers, lovers, spouses, family members, church, and temple associates.

Still, I remained conflicted about being a healer, often feeling like a fraud who would soon be discovered as a charlatan. Who was I to be working with other people in this capacity when I still had so much emotional work to do? I detested the word healer. I wasn't the one doing the healing. I never referred to myself as one and searched for a word I could live with. I finally rested on body worker. In those days, there weren't a lot of us in NYC. Many masseurs were actually hookers. When I told people I was a body worker, most people, especially men, would cock their head to the left, grin and say, "I've never met a mechanic that looked like you." They thought they were funny and slick. I thought they were rude, ignorant and unoriginal.

Underneath my anger, the truth was that I felt humiliated, ostracized and grief stricken. If it had been up to my personality self (aka my ego), I would never have become a healer. I would have been a famous anything, you name it, actress, singer, stand-up comic, writer or even a successful VP of a major company. Any would have sufficed. But healer, no thank you.

Everywhere I went, I met healers who identified me as one of them. The synchronicity was eerie. During a walk through Central Park one day, I bumped into a group of people dressed in purple garb, with one man in maroon. I figured that they were a Hare Krishna sect. As children, we were warned never to talk with them or even go near them. They often hung out at The Commonwealth Park in downtown Boston. It was also a favorite place for teens. My parents warned us that they were part of a cult that brainwashed children and took them away from their parents.

The Indian men gathered around the man in maroon, and many people began surrounding this group. I recognized one of them as the actor, Richard Gere. Two men, one in the maroon garb and one in navy blue and gold stood looking in my direction. I was so drawn to them, I walked directly towards them. I found myself standing right in front of the man in a maroon robe. He said something to the other man in a language I didn't understand or recognize. Smiling he said, "You have much work to do. We will meet again at another time."

"Thank you," I said and smiled back, even though I was thinking, "What the hell does this mean? And who are you people?"

As they walked away, my heart was beating rapidly. His words had power, even though I didn't understand the meaning of them. Years later, I saw a picture of Richard Gere with the man I had met in Central Park. It was the Dalai Lama.

Part of what scared me about the message was that somewhere deep inside I could feel the truth of what he said. I knew we would meet again. And I knew that Jeffrey would not be with me. I could no longer shake off this truth.

At this point, my marriage was in deep danger. I had been in therapy for four years trying to understand my marriage. Was it me? Was it Jeffrey? I didn't know. Once I understood that it was our dynamic, I spent two years trying to find the courage to leave our marriage, to disobey my father and to devastate Jeffrey. I knew I needed to leave in order to mature and discover my own power.

When Jeffrey and I weren't fighting, we attempted to be civil. We'd carry on daily life, eating dinners together, and attempting to have fun on weekends. Even though I was physically there, I began to leave the marriage, creating a separate life for myself. Six months prior to leaving, I moved out of our bedroom and began sleeping in the backroom.

I interviewed three reputable lawyers that had been recommended to me. They approached divorces with vampire-like zeal. None of them were spiritual. The last lawyer was a tall thin woman with long red fingernails that almost curled. For 30 minutes, she tapped her fingernails on her desk while describing her heartless, kill mentality. When I left her office, I knew that above all else, I wanted a fair divorce. I didn't want blood money or to "break" my husband's world.

In late September, I told Jeffrey. He grabbed the play I'd been writing on my typewriter for over a year entitled, "Orbiting Paradise," and ripped it to shreds. He raged that he wouldn't make it easy for me to get a divorce, screaming, "You made a promise. You promised to be my wife forever. Doesn't that mean anything to you?"

I stood shocked at his emotion. What he said was true. I couldn't deny it, but I had made a promise at 21, well before I knew who I was. I now needed to find out who I was.

To have a fair divorce, we settled upon a mediator. She tried to be fair to me, but I was clueless about how much it cost to live well in New York City and naive about how fast my healing practice would grow. And I wanted to prove that I could support myself and stand on my own two feet. We settled on $61,000 to be paid out over the course of three years. A mere pittance for what Jeffrey made as a certified tax attorney in a private practice representing CEOs and multimillionaires. But it seemed a small price to pay for my liberation.

The rest of my family was responding in their own fashion to my father's death. Robert, enraged by the lack of a financial legacy from my father, ran back to his wife and two boys in Florida. It would be years before I ever spoke to him again. Michael, remaining true to himself, said very little and returned home to his daily life as a hard-working commercial realtor, dutiful husband and father to his two children. Jessa continued in her teaching position and would soon fall in love and get married. Brian went back to school where he was studying business. As far as I knew, except for Jessa, none of my siblings were doing any personal healing to overcome the trauma of our childhood. After the funeral, we all went our own way. For the most part, we all dealt with Dad's death in silence and with our friends.

For the first few months after my father's death, my mother appeared to be doing remarkably well. I spoke to her daily from New York City and was surprised that she had made the transition so easily. I wondered what she would do when the money she received from my father ran out, but her attitude was optimistic. Each week however, her new optimism began to feel more manic. During our conversations, I would ask her how she was really doing and her response was always the same, "I'm fine. Don't worry, Ellen. I'm fine."

I should have known better than to believe her, but I needed to believe her. If she could stand on her own two feet, then I could too. What I couldn't see was that she had begun medicating herself with a bottle of wine each night. Slowly, her manic tone worsened. Had I seen her, I would have known she was on a downward cycle. I knew that look from years of watching her cycle through depression. Somewhere deep inside me, I think I knew she was not doing well, but was too emotionally drained to deal with her. A little more than one year after my father died, my mother had a psychotic breakdown. She was hospitalized. Even though we spoke often by phone, I didn't go and visit her. For my own developmental growth and sanity, I needed to take my space away from her.

One Sunday, less than six months after my divorce from Jeffrey, I was catching up on laundry and returning phone calls to friends. I had just moved from my walk-up studio into an apartment on Riverside drive. It was a happy space, large windows with a southern exposure overlooked the park where children ran and giggled. The phone rang and echoed in the sparse apartment.

"Hello?"

"Ellen, what are you doing?" my brother Michael demanded. Before I could answer, he rambled on, "Do you realize how sick Mom is? What are you going to do?"

Fury rose in my body, but I tried remaining calm. Of course, I realized how sick she was. I was the one observing her for the past thirty-one years and warning my father of her impending depressions and breakdowns.

"Michael, I am not going to do anything," I said in a measured manner. "She is in the hospital so that people can take good care of her. That's what they are there to do."

"How could you just leave her like this, Ellen? What is wrong with you?"

How could I explain five years of therapy in one conversation? How could I relay to him how difficult this decision had been to make? It was breaking my heart daily. I wasn't sleeping and had to force myself to eat. Every day, I questioned my sanity and my therapist's sanity. My therapist explained that in order to end my chronic co-dependency and to learn how to stop merging with my mother, I needed to keep my distance from her. It was nearly impossible. I swung between existential guilt and fear, and a longing and thirst for my mother. I wanted and needed to be by her side. My therapist argued that it was my addicted, sick self that felt this way, and if I was to ever achieve a semblance of balance I needed to take this opportunity and cut the umbilical cord once and for all. Most of my days, I was consumed by sheer terror. How could my mother be okay without me? I imagined the phone ringing with a stranger's voice on the other end informing me that my mother was dead. I could barely eat, breathe or sleep. How could I explain to him that it was the hardest decision I had ever made? It was the first time I'd said no since I was 14 and found her lying on our living room floor from an overdose. How could I explain that I was scared to death to let my mother go and scared not to?

"Michael, listen to me for a second, would you, please? Do you think this is easy for me?"

"Then why the fuck are you doing this to her? She needs you."

"No, that's where you're wrong, Michael. She needs herself!"

"Ellen, she's psychotic. Don't you get it? Psy-chotic."

I had not heard my brother this vocal since he was a little kid. "Michael, you might not understand this, but I am doing this based on my therapist's professional advice." My brother and I had gone different routes. He stuffed all of his emotions. I went to therapy. Michael believed in hard work and silence. I believed in understanding and expressing my emotions as a way to live a sane existence. I couldn't believe I was laying the "professional" card out there but I was not yet strong enough to hold my own. I had too many of my own doubts.

"And what does your fucking therapist know about Mom and us!"

"She knows enough to know that she needs to find her own strength and way in the world."

He laughed cynically. "Ellen, all she does is cry all day, and she believes everyone is out to get her. Does that sound like a person who can find their own strength? I think your therapist is fucking delusional." He was beginning to sound just like the man he hated, our dad.

"Michael, I need to do this. I need to have my own life."

"We all need our own life, but we don't get to have that, do we? Ellen, she's gone fucking crazy."

I took a deep breath and repeated my therapist's words. "And maybe that's exactly what she needs to do to heal."

"Heal? Heal? What the fuck do you know about healing? Your own mother needs you and all you can do is turn your back on her. You call that healing? You're just a fuckin' selfish bitch!"

There was silence. I didn't know what else to say, and I was weakening from his repeated blows.

"If she dies, it'll be on your head."

"Michael…"

He pounced on my words, "Don't fuckin' call me. Don't ever call me!"

"Michael…"

"I hope you never need someone. I hope you fucking get yours someday, you fucking selfish bitch."

"Mi…"

"Don't ever call me. Don't ever fuckin' call me your brother."

There was a dead empty silence, and then I heard the click as he hung up. I tried calling him back five times, managing only to reach his cheery voice mail.

"Leave a message and I'll call you right back." He never did.

Healer

My father's death, my mother's breakdown. My divorce, a brother's rage. Death, loss, grieving. I often felt barely tethered to this world. On the other side of my grief, there was the birth of my healing practice. A flow of energy grounded me, offering me purpose, supporting me and my patients' spiritual and emotional growth. Light graced the darkness, allowing me to open and blossom.

After a year as a healer, I began to realize that my patients often reflected my own issues and challenges. Session after session, in my work with Donna, I witnessed a young woman emerging out of her cocoon of suffering. As the helpless victim, she bore a startling resemblance to the mother of my childhood. Even though Donna had grown enormously in our year working together, she was still battling many demons.

One day, she called to schedule an emergency session. I wondered if she had broken up with the latest boyfriend. She arrived fifteen minutes early. I had a cancellation and was able to begin the session early. Without taking her coat off, she plunked herself down in the brown leather chair in my office.

"I fucked up," she said looking at the floor. "I don't deserve to be a mother, especially not Miranda's mother." She began sobbing as if she, herself, were the five-year-old child.

My stomach flipped and flopped. Donna's words were too familiar. Her voice sounded like my mother's. I took a deep breath. I needed to be here with Donna – not with my little girl or with my mother. Inside, I said to all of my inner children, "This is not our mother, and I, the adult, will handle this."

Donna curled up into a ball, crumbling under the pressure of her emotional pain. "I want you to take a deep breath," I said, "And see if you can make eye contact with me."

She shook her head.

"Donna, have you hurt Miranda physically?"

She shook her head no.

"Okay, my dear, take a deep breath and when you can, I'd like you to tell me what happened."

She began shaking. After a moment, she lifted her head and made eye contact with me. Her eyes were frozen with fear. I couldn't help but to see my own mother's eyes.

"Donna, whatever has happened we can work through this." She began sobbing and speaking, but I couldn't make sense out of her garbled sobs. I waited.

"Miranda deserves a better mother," she said slowly with her head held down. "I'm just no good for her."

"Donna, you give Miranda so much love. And you have grown so much over this last year. I see enormous growth. I can't imagine a better mother for such a creative, spirited child like Miranda."

She looked up at me and into my eyes as if asking, do you really mean that?

"That is the truth, my dear. I can't imagine a better mother for her, truly."

Donna was a very young mother it was true, but she was also a devoted mother. She loved Miranda with all her heart.

What she may have lacked in emotional maturity, she made up for in pure love.

When she was able to speak, she explained what had happened. She'd been looking through her journal entries over the past year and realized for the first time, that she was in her own words, "a complete mess". She was shocked at her own writing and her own life. I could see that Donna had entered a new phase of healing. "Yes," I said. "As a person's awareness grows, one's deficits become more evident. This stage of healing holds the potential for enormous self-judgment. It's a delicate balancing act to see one's deficiencies and not descend into self-loathing."

I was so proud of her for getting to this place, and yet I knew how painful this part of the process was.

"Let's take this grief to the table."

As soon as Donna lay down on her back, I placed my left hand behind her heart and my right hand above her heart. Although Donna often resembled my mother, knowing she was not, allowed me to be fully present with her and her pain. But at times, I could still feel my mind being pulled towards my own mother's story. Like Donna, my mother suffered from a debilitating depression as a young woman. They both lacked enough self-esteem to support themselves financially and emotionally. Addicted to men, they were certain the only way to have financial security was by having a man support them.

Unlike Donna, however, my mother was never afforded true therapy. She'd been treated in a time when women were often subjected to cruel therapies, administered shock treatment while awake. Donna was blessed to be of a younger generation that didn't see depression as some curse of God or the devil or just another woman being crazy, but rather as a real medical condition that needed to be treated as any other illness would be.

Witnessing the many similarities between Donna and my mother allowed me to view my mother from a different perspective. I was able to see my mother more as another human being having her own experience separate from me as her daughter. Even though I continued to struggle with issues surrounding my mother, I came to have more compassion for her as a young woman with little or no support muddling her way through depression, anxiety and terror. It took the edge off of the hatred I still felt towards her. Through Donna's eyes, I came to understand why my mother was never able to be present for me when I was a young girl. I still struggled, however, to understand how she could have allowed my father to treat me as he did.

As my work with Donna grew, I came to understand the position and mindset my mother had been in. While I still fought hard to accept her submissive position with my father, my compassion for her grew. As my heart opened to Donna, the sheer disappointment, disgust and disgrace I felt towards my mother lessened. She was, after all, a wounded young girl suffering from depression who had grown up to become an abused woman with severe mental illness. And this too was hard for me to accept. I wanted the brilliant mother who I could see, to show me my path as a woman.

Holding Donna's feet, I could feel that she had finally settled back into her body.

"Take a deep breath," I said, "Breathe in the light of safety. Breathe in the light of courage." I watched as her breath deepened into her belly and listened as she sighed.

"Excellent. Take your time, and when you're ready, you can sit up."

When Donna sat up I was amazed to see how much her face had softened. Her eyes had even lost some of their haunting quality reminiscent of Holocaust victims' eyes.

"How are you feeling?" I asked.

"Better, but still a little shaky." Taking a deep breath, staring straight into my eyes she asked, "Do you really think I can be a good mother to Miranda?"

"Yes, I do. You, my dear, are the perfect mother for Miranda. Perfectly, imperfect."

A laugh escaped Donna's mouth, catching us both off guard.

I laughed along with her and gave her a hug. "You are the perfect mother for Miranda, just perfect."

In that year, many new patients were referred to me by Donna's therapist, her psychiatrist, and by other patients. I was constantly amazed at how often these patients' issues mirrored my own. None, however, matched the intensity of Donna.

When Sarina, an independently wealthy Swiss woman, first came to see me, it appeared at first glance that she had everything in the world. She had legs I could only dream about. They were nearly the length of my entire body. She looked like a cross between a well-oiled marathon runner and an elegant heiress of old aristocratic stock.

I had to admit I was jealous. As I listened to her story, I could feel my cheeks blushing with desire for the kind of wealth and family life that I imagined Sarina had. I knew that to be a healing guide for Sarina I would need to work through my own jealousies.

In my healing process, I realized that what I was longing for was not necessarily Sarina's money, but the security and comfort I'd imagined her to have due to a vast endowment from her family. Within a few sessions, it became clear that Sarina, like all of us, had many of her own issues to work on in order to heal, and have a fulfilled, soulful life.

As my jealousy subsided, I began to see that Sarina's long, thin arms hung lifeless by her side. And even though she always wore a big smile, her eyes belied it, possessing a sad empty quality. During our fourth session, as hard as she tried to contain herself, a flood of emotions erupted. It shocked this lovely young woman of aristocratic stock to be this unruly. In the midst of this emotional upheaval, she looked up at me as if to ask if this was permissible. From a very young age, she had been reared to suppress her emotions, as they were not tolerated in her household.

As we worked together, Sarina came to learn many truths about her family history that had been masked by the family's wealth and international acclaim. Unearthing her truth, she came to understand that her deep yearning to be a mother was, in part, to give a child the warmth and love she had never received. First, though, she needed to fulfill her own longing and heal her own inner child.

She began to have childhood memories of speaking with angels in her bedroom. Her heart longed to reconnect with them. A calling to facilitate other people through their healing journeys grew within her. She entered a full-time, two-year program to become a certified Energy Healer. She found it nurturing to assist other people in their healing. It prepared her for motherhood. A year later, Sarina birthed her first child, a son, into warm water.

Unlike a lot of psychics I had gone to, the information I channeled was direct, practical and down-to-earth. My spirit guides did not waste their energy on flowery platitudes. They offered simple and precise steps for the greatest healing. The difficulty came in one's willingness to follow the information, as it almost always led people out of their comfort zones. The more I worked with my guides, the more amazed I was at the consistent accuracy of their information despite my own skepticism.

The guides I came to know as The Board worked through me with great compassion. They also worked with great clarity and direct speech. I often wanted to smooth things and change their language as I found it too direct, harsh and on the edge of being mean. They reassured me that because their intent was to heal, and they came from a truly compassionate place, what they had to say would be heard through that lens, no matter how difficult. Every time I softened what they had said, it never went well. My patients either grew confused or worse; they became incensed. I learned to be a good stenographer and leave my own thoughts and ego out.

Despite the consistent, uncanny accuracy and wisdom of my guides, I continued to struggle against my own emergent psychic abilities. These experiences often ebbed too close to the edge of what I had witnessed during my mother's psychotic breakdowns. Could I hold that kind of power or my budding joy, I wondered, and remain tethered to the earth — to reality — and to my own sanity?

Delores had come to me for a pain located deep in her buttock dealing with a small muscle called the piriformis. She had been playing bridge with friends and all she remembered was sneezing as she reached forward to advance her game. A hot, searing pain shot through her left buttock all the way down her left leg and foot. She went to see her doctor who sent her to a pain specialist. Through tests, he surmised it was the piriformis muscle causing the pain. He sent her to a doctor who specialized in issues of the piriformis muscle. After receiving treatments for a few weeks, she remained in a great deal of agony.

As I was worked with her, in my hands-on energy fashion, my guides told me to put the sound of an E in her lower abdomen. In all my time working with them, they had never suggested I sing a vowel into someone's body. I absolutely denied their request. They had gone too far. Using my voice for healing seemed ludicrous. Nor did I have a good enough voice to croon in public.

In high contrast, when my father sang in public, people would stop him and ask where he performed. His deep voice was captivating. Ever since I was a young girl, as far back as I could remember, I had secretly wanted to be a singer and to have the sonorous voice of my father. I feared I'd inherited, however, the nasally, tone-deaf voice of my mother.

The thought of singing into someone's body seemed crazy to me, even dangerous. I was irritated my guides had the audacity to suggest it.

At the end of Dolores' session, I had a mild headache. It became scorching and lasted much of that night. In subsequent sessions with Delores and other clients, my guides continued to insist that I put sound into their bodies. I resisted, and I continued to get headaches. After a few months of living daily with the pain, I made the connection between my guides' request to use my voice and my resistance. Finally, exhausted, I followed their guidance at the next session.

Mitch was a successful Wall Street executive, who was addicted to cocaine. My guides suggested I tone an Ah vowel into Mitch's heart. How would Mitch react to this weird use of sound? Would it do something strange to him? Would he ever return for another session? I calmly explained to Mitch what I was going to do at the behest of my guides and asked him if he was game. Mitch was desperate to get clean and sober. He was willing to do just about anything to heal. I took a deep breath, put my left hand under his heart on his back and my right hand on top of his heart, leaned down and sang an Ah. To my amazement, Mitch began to cry like a little boy. I was not prepared for this strong reaction, but knew to hold the space. When he could speak, he said, "Ellen, how did you do that?"

"Do what?"

"Your song sounded just like my mom's voice. When I was

a little boy and afraid of the dark, she'd come into my room and rub my back and sing me a lullaby that sounded just like that."

Mitch's mother had committed suicide when he was 15. I was speechless. Once again my guides provided exactly the right medicine for my client's healing.

During the following year, session after session, my guides showed me how to utilize sound for healing. I often resisted. It made no sense to me, and I felt too vulnerable singing non-sensical sounds into people's bodies. Still, I did as they requested, putting the sound of an Ah into Shuli's stomach, an E into Debra's knee and an O into Mark's heart chakra. Each time, I was both relieved and amazed at how perfectly resonant the sound was for each person's healing.

Working with my patients and on myself, I came to appreciate that doing emotional and spiritual work to heal doesn't give us a Free Pass card. It doesn't mean that everything goes our way. We still have daily ups and downs. But we'll have better skills and tools to work through our life's challenges. As I came into a deeper alignment with myself and my spirit, I realized that it wouldn't necessarily translate into attaining more worldly goodies such as monetary success or fame. But I began to experience more joy and happiness than I had ever imagined.

Seeing the difference I made in my patients' lives delighted and thrilled me. The deeper we worked together, the more I understood how my own suffering had prepared me to be able to sit with my patient's suffering in a deep soulful, non-judgmental manner that was far beyond the wisdom of my chronological years. Without my life challenges, I could never have truly understood their pain and held the kind of sacred space that was required for their healing. The pain and atrocities I had survived finally had purpose. And through it all, my heart was softening and opening. I was learning to love myself.

Second to helping others to heal, my other greatest joy and

achievement was living on my own. I rented a walk-up apartment on 108th street. The entire apartment was smaller than the front foyer in the apartment on 86th I shared with Jeffrey. When I sat on the toilet, my knees were practically in the middle of the kitchen. I didn't care. For the first time in my life, I was free to say anything, do anything and be anyone I wanted to be. And yet, with my newfound freedom, fear storms accompanied me on most days. My longstanding fear of becoming one of Manhattan's toothless bag ladies plagued me nightly. I feared ending up like my mother or worse, losing her. My father's voice resounded in my mind constantly reminding me that the only women who supported themselves were angry divorcees or dikes. Defenseless to these ungrounded machinations, my body battled these ensuing threats until I was devoured by panic, certain I was a breath away from reliving my mother's fate.

As I lay in my new bed alone, May Day, May 1, 1991, I shook with fear, wondering if Jeffrey would ever take me back. Rather than feeling the joy of freedom, I felt the sting of being single. Death seemed to be lurking in the shadows. Hour after hour, I replayed my father's and mother's voices.

"Ellen, so help me God, I'm gonna throw her out of the house if she doesn't turn around. She'll be out on the street, if you don't do something."

"I can't leave. I don't have any money. I couldn't support you kids."

"Women need to be supported. The only women that support themselves are gay, or divorcees. Even they are just using their husband's money to support themselves."

"Ellen, I can't be on my own. How would I ever support myself?"

The memory of my mother sitting at the edge of my bed, dragging on her Salems and crying about how she could never leave my father because she would end up on the streets, invaded my psyche. On each breath, I prayed to make it through the night. Awaiting dawn, I grieved the end of my marriage, my father's death, and the annihilation of the deep-seated truths ingrained into me by my parents.

Slowly, I began to take ownership of my new home by decorating it. I found three toilet bowls on the street and a homeless man named Floyd willing to carry them up four flights of stairs for five bucks. Climbing through the only window in the sitting room, I had him place them on the outdoor landing. The toilets were the foundation of my outdoor garden. Filled with geraniums, petunias and impatiens, they made a fascinating conversation piece. Inside, I adorned the sitting room with found objects from street fairs and early morning walks throughout Manhattan. A hubcap, a Coca Cola bottle from Mexico with a bright orange and yellow woven base, a wooden walking stick someone had carved into a beak, and an old typewriter, turned the narrow pale white sitting room, that doubled as my treatment room by day, into a collage of vibrant colors: orange, reds and deep earthen tones, each infused with magical stories.

After the first few months on my own, my fears began to subside, exposing unresolved grief that lived below the surface. I grieved for my mother who never found her own voice or her power. I grieved for myself, the young girl who had been subjected to all of my parent's crazy ideas, dysfunctional and violent behavior. I grieved that it had taken me so long to learn to care for myself financially and emotionally. Knowing that I had to show up for my patients each day offered me a great safety net. It allowed me to go down into the depths of my dark underworld, knowing I would be lifted to the light by morning.

In my grieving, I debunked one of our modern day myths, that life should always be easy. It simply was not. Month after month of intense emotional and spiritual self-work, I wondered where the payoff was. I soon discovered that my way of looking at spiritual work was still through childish lenses. Healing our wounded hearts and souls is the payoff. And the greatest "prize", if you will, is in living wholly from your inner core, from your own integrity.

Slowly, I gained a new self-confidence, an emerging empowerment. My own freedom was echoed in my clients.

During one of her regular weekly sessions in May 1992, Donna announced, "I'm going to do it. I'm finally going to support myself and Miranda financially. I think it's time for me to do it. Even though I've fought you on this, I've always known you were right. I just wasn't ready. I think I'm finally ready."

My heart filled with joy. "This is wonderful," I said, beaming inside myself. "How are you planning on doing this?"

"I'm going to go to massage school and become a massage therapist."

Tears flooded my eyes; I couldn't hold them back. I flashed back to Donna's first session with her curled up like a ball in the chair across from me. She had come so far.

"Where are you thinking of going?"

"I'm going to go to school in California. There's a school in Santa Monica. I can get financial aid to get me through the program, so I can also be with Miranda."

Donna had always dreamed of going to California. I just didn't know if she'd ever make it there. "That is perfect. How does Miranda feel about it?"

"She's totally excited and scared."

"That would be just about right."

"She's asked if she can come and see you before we leave."

"Of course, I wouldn't have it any other way."

In early September, the day of their move, Donna and Miranda arrived at my office at 7 a.m. Donna, with her silky blond hair, tight, washed out blue jeans, and red high top sneakers, looked like a young woman ready to go off to college for the first time. Miranda wore a sparkling purple dress over pink leggings, a furry chocolate brown vest, and a pair of brown leather boots rounded off her outfit. She looked like she had just stepped right out of a Gap Kids back-to-school catalogue.

Without warning, Miranda jumped into my arms, almost knocking me over.

"I have a secret," she whispered. "You'll always be my best friend."

I could have crumpled into a heap of tears. Instead I tickled her and made up a song and sang it to her, "Miranda, the pretty little girl with long brown curls, and a heart of gold, has glued my heart to hers forever and ever. Miranda, the pretty little girl with long brown curls…"

"You ready?" I said tapping her on the nose.

She scrunched her shoulders up. "Yeah, sort of."

"What's the sort of not part?"

"What if I get afraid of the dark in our new place?" she whispered.

My eyes fell upon one of my most treasured possessions, a popple rock; a rock that looks like a big giant egg. They are formed and actually get their name from the tumbling or the poppling, as it used to be called, from ocean water forced into small coves. I stumbled upon such a small cove, measuring just 5 feet long in length, a few summers earlier up in Maine.

I grabbed the rock off of my bookshelf and held it tightly in the palm of my hand and breathed. Unfolding my hand to reveal this majestic creature, I said, "This is not your ordinary rock. An angel lives inside this rock. And she especially likes children. Whenever you feel scared, just hold her and whisper to her, she'll be there to help you. This is a very special rock to me. And I think it's perfect that it's going to go home with such a special little girl."

Her powdery blue eyes lit up. She looked over at her mom. Donna nodded her head.

"Really?" she said to me. "You're really going to give her to me?"

"Yes, I think she was meant for you." I closed my eyes and squeezed the rock deeply. "Yes, I can feel that she's happy to go home with you, too. See if you can feel that," I said, handing the rock to Miranda. Can you feel her warmth?"

"Yes," she answered softly. "She feels just like you, especially when you sing."

Her words broke my heart wide open. I grabbed her and her mom for a group bear hug.

"I will miss you guys." Pulling far enough apart so I could look into Donna's eyes, I said, "I'm so proud of you. You've done good, my dear. You've done very, very good."

"Thank you," Donna whispered through her tears. "Thank you for everything."

"It has been my joy. Now go," I said. "And let me know how you're doing."

Donna and Miranda turned and left my office. Watching them from my window, climbing into their U-Haul, a sense of awe rolled through my entire being at the resilience and possibility of healing that exists within all of us. I flashed back to my first meeting with Donna, just two years earlier. She had arrived at my office looking like a translucent waif with shocked laden eyes, trembling. She was scarcely bound to her body or the earth. Witnessing Donna leave with her new acquired strength and her daughter in hand, I knew we had laid the path of generational healing for years to come.

With their U-Haul now fully out of sight, alone in the silence, I felt an echo back to those difficult days of my own healing.

Just three years earlier, I was hanging onto the metal pole in the middle of the E train for dear life, feeling barely tethered to this world myself. I could hardly have imagined living this life, doing soul-fulfilling work. I was grateful to have overcome so much adversity in such a relatively short span of time. With so much practical and sacred guidance, I had faced some of my darkest fears and demons with the courage and fierceness of a true warrior.

Standing at the window, I no longer felt like a tiny boat strewn about by turbulent fear currents. Wisdom and compassion now charted my course. Waves of gratitude and humility washed over me, blessed to be a healing force for others, assisting them to recover their own light.

Pondering my own journey and Donna's, I knew healing was possible for anyone who'd take themselves seriously enough to devote their time, attention and energy to the emotional and spiritual journey offered to them. While not an easy path, it was a worthy one. Treacherous at times, with days, even weeks and months where I questioned my own sanity for staying with the healing process, the path was also immensely rewarding.

I knew beyond any reasonable doubt that if I hadn't accepted my healing path, I would have, at the very least, become far sicker. Living a life that wasn't in alignment with my highest self, I would've been plagued with mental disorders, such as the severe panic attacks I had been besieged with. Or worse, I would have died. On the other side of darkness, I had met the light.

Piercing the veil of consciousness, I now looked toward the future with great wonder and expectancy. I knew the next phase of my personal and spiritual development would be found in my willingness to continue to stand on my own two feet, both emotionally and financially. I walked away from everything I had been taught was acceptable forms of work, by my parents, my educational upbringing, and my Jewish culture. Breaking free of cultural expectations and norms was not enough. I now needed to take further ownership of myself as healer, and stop hiding behind self-deprecating humor and my ubiquitous smile. I had to be willing to not fit in.

Through the first portal, I had met, fought and overcome many of love's adversaries. As I glimpsed into the future, I saw that my greatest healing would come when I summoned up the courage to enter into a fully committed relationship, nourished by an unselfish, yielding love. Love had become my teacher and would be my ultimate healer.

Little did I know, the next step on the journey would take me thousands of miles away to an ashram in southern India where the putrid smells of raw sewage would swarm alive my dulled senses and a love so cunning would cut my heart wide open with a surgeon's precision.

Ellen Newhouse loves sharing her creative voice through her writing, singing and healing. She has a thriving healing practice in Seattle, WA where she integrates Acupuncture, Sound Healing, Energy Medicine and Intuitive Coaching. She loves empowering her patients to live fully in their power, in their passion and in their voice. In addition to her private practice, she teaches workshops throughout the United States and has appeared on numerous radio shows. Ellen enjoys sharing her laughter as well as her insights. Ellen and her husband Jim enjoy the raw beauty of the Northwest and the eclectic city of Seattle. It's a great place to write...and sing your heart out!

Visit her website at **www.ellennewhouse.com**

Resources

National Hotlines

National Domestic Violence Hotline
Staffed 24 hours a day by trained counselors who can provide crisis assistance and information about shelters, legal advocacy, health care centers, and counseling.
1-800-799-SAFE (7233)
1-800-787-3224 (TDD)

National Center on Domestic and Sexual Violence: A national training organization, NCDSV works to influence national policy and provides customized training and consultation to professionals working in fields that might influence domestic violence.

National Domestic Violence Hotline: The Hotline provides 24-hour support and crisis intervention to victims and survivors of DV through safety planning, advocacy, resources, and a supportive ear.

Rape, Abuse, and Incest National Network (RAINN): RAINN is the nation's largest anti-sexual violence organization. The Network created and operates the National Sexual Assault Hotline (800.656.HOPE) and operates the Department of Defense's Safe Helpline. The organization also runs programs to prevent sexual violence, assist survivors, and ensure that rapists are brought to justice.

V-Day: Founded by author Eve Ensler and activists from New York City, V-Day is a global activist movement seeking to end violence against women and girls. The organization stages creative events—most famously, *The Vagina Monologues* and the documentary *Until the Violence Stops* —to increase awareness, raise funds, and support other anti-violence organizations.

Jewish Women International: JWI seeks to empower women and girls through economic literacy, community trainings, and education about healthy relationships. The organization aims to end violence against women by advocating for policies focused on violence prevention and reproductive rights, developing philanthropic initiatives along similar lines, and inspiring "the next generation of leaders" by recognizing and celebrating women's achievements.

National Latino Alliance for the Elimination of Domestic Violence (ALIANZA): Allianza is a network of organizations addressing the needs of Latino/a families and communities by promoting understanding, dialogue, and solutions that aim to eliminate domestic violence in Latino communities.

The Northwest Network: Founded by lesbian survivors of domestic, the NW Network works to end abuse in lesbian, gay, bisexual, and transgender communities and to support and empower all survivors through education and advocacy.

INCITE! Women of Color Against Violence: INCITE! describes itself as a "national activist organization of radical feminists of color advancing a movement to end violence against women of color and our communities." Comprised of grassroots chapters across the U.S., the organization works with groups of women of color and their communities to develop political projects that address the violence women of color may experience both within their communities and individual lives.

Asian & Pacific Islander Institute on Domestic Violence: The API Institute is a national resource center focused on gender-based violence (DV, sexual violence, and trafficking) in Asian and Pacific Islander communities. It addresses these issues by increasing awareness, strengthening community strategies for prevention and intervention, and promoting research and policy.

Hot Peach Pages: Worldwide list of Agencies Against Domestic Violence Website: www.hotpeachpages.net

How To Help — Your Action Plan

Want to help out? Start by getting in touch with any of the organizations listed above; they can point you to volunteer opportunities across the country. We've also put together a list of other ways to show support:

- Commit to the National Domestic Violence Hotline's 20 Challenges for Change.

- Write to your favorite companies and ask them to support domestic violence programs with their philanthropic funds.

- Be a source of support. Learn how to speak to and help friends, family members, or acquaintances who come to you with stories of violence.

- Talk about it. Educate yourself about domestic violence and pass along the knowledge to friends and family. Things change much faster when we direct our energies to changing them.

Therapeutic Resources

National Certification Commission for Acupuncture and Oriental Medicine: http://www.nccaom.org/find-a-nccaom-certified-practitioner This is a wonderful resource to find a certified Acupuncturist in your hometown to help your body, mind and spirit to heal.

Psychology Today Therapist:
http://therapists.psychologytoday.com/rms/
This will give you a good starting point to find a certified therapist.

Women to Women: http://www.womentowomen.com/clinic/
This is a wonderful resource for women's medical questions and concerns. As part of your healing journey, it is essential to take good care of your body and your gynecological health.

Art of Storytelling: http://www.artofstorytelling.com
Caroline Allen
Writing your story can be a powerful healing tool. Carrie has an amazing ability to guide people through the fears and judgments about writing to recovering their authentic voice through the writing process.

Karen Glass
Website is: www.GlassMassage.com
Karen has a rare gift to assist people in their healing journey.
I highly recommend her!

Leslie Gifford
lesliejgifford@gmail.com
Astrologer
Leslie has quite a talent in helping people to see their lives from a fresh perspective as well as an uncanny gift in guiding people onto their soul path.

CPSIA information can be obtained at www.ICGtesting.com
Printed in the USA
BVOW05s2010121014

370516BV00001B/1/P